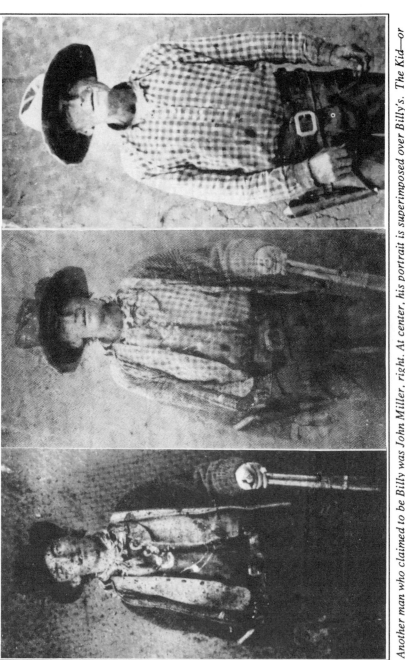

Another man who claimed to be Billy was John Miller, right. At center, his portrait is superimposed over Billy's. The Kid—or an impostor? Smithsonian Magazine, February, 1991.

WHATEVER HAPPENED TO BILLY THE KID?

Helen Airy

SUNSTONE
PRESS

Dedicated to Fred Airy

First Edition

Printed in the United States of America

_____

Library of Congress Cataloging in Publication Data:
Airy, Helen, 1914-
    Whatever happened to Billy the Kid / by Helen Airy. — 1st ed.
        p. cm.
    ISBN 0-86534-185-0 : $12.95
    1. Billy, the Kid—Death and burial. 2. Outlaws—Southwest,
    New Biography. I.Title
    F786.B54A35   1992
    364. 1'552'0921—dc20   92-9629
    [B]   CIP

_____

Published by: SUNSTONE PRESS
                     Post Office Box 2321
                     Santa Fe, NM 87504-2321 / USA

Cover design by Patrick DeAloe

CONTENTS

Foreword

Tales From Ramah and Buckeye

John Miller's attempts to keep his neighbors in the Ramah-Zuni area from knowing he was Billy the Kid were somewhat less than successful. Just about everybody out there knew that John Miller was Billy the Kid. Today you can still find a few survivors who knew John Miller personally, all of whom say they knew all the time that John Miller was Billy the Kid. There are many more who are descendants of people who knew John Miller, all of whom will tell you their relatives told them that John Miller was Billy the Kid.

Ask any of these people the question: "Do you think John Miller was Billy the Kid?"

Invariably they will reply: "Of course Miller was Billy the Kid. Didn't you know that?"

You might answer meekly: "No, I didn't know that. How do you know that?"

Some will say: "Miller told me he was Billy the Kid."

Some will say: "Miller's wife told me he was Billy the Kid."

Some will say: "Miller's son, Max, told me Miller was Billy the Kid."

Others might say: "Miller's friend Herman Tecklenburg, who knew Miller in Fort Sumner when Miller was known as Billy the Kid, told me."

Most people will say: "Everyone knew that John Miller was Billy the Kid."

That last, "everyone knew," will put you in your place, because you didn't know. Don't worry, you're in good company. Over the past 110 years Billy the Kid buffs, authorities of all kinds including historians, writers, movie makers and other important people, haven't known that John Miller was Billy the Kid. Even now it's hard for some people to believe that the Kid was not killed by Pat Garrett, but survived to live a long life as a rancher in the Zuni Mountains in McKinley County, New Mexico, and was known as John Miller.

Meet some of the people who knew John Miller and some who were told that John Miller was Billy the Kid:

John Miller's adopted son, Max Miller, Herman Tecklenburg, John Herman Tecklenburg, Eugene Lambson, Atheling Bond, Wilfred Ashcroft, Bertha Ashcroft, Bill Crockett, Jewel Crockett Lambson, Feliz Bustamante, Blanche Lewis, Frank Burrard Creasy, Andrew Vander Wagen, Effa Vander Wagen, Gary Tietjen, Joe Tietjen, Jesus Eriacho, Katherine Eriacho, Keith Clawson, Sheryl Clawson and Wayne Clawson. And from Buckeye, Arizona: Ethel Conley, Joe Conley, and Carl Baxter.

All of these people have told their stories about Billy the Kid, whom they knew as John Miller. Their stories have been recorded in the pages of this book. As many as possible have been taped. Most of the people who knew John Miller personally were in their late eighties or early nineties when they were interviewed. Trying to remember events that occurred eighty years ago was not easy. As a result, there are some minor discrepancies in their stories. The author has not changed anything that was said. They were all doing their best to remember correctly.

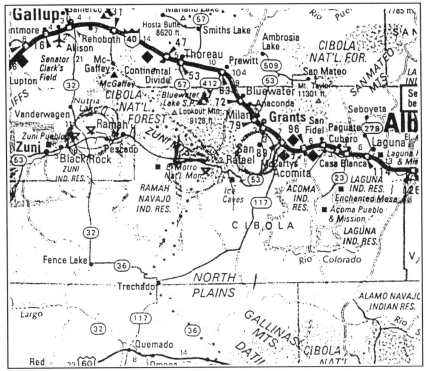

Western New Mexico where John Miller spent most of his life as a cattle rancher.

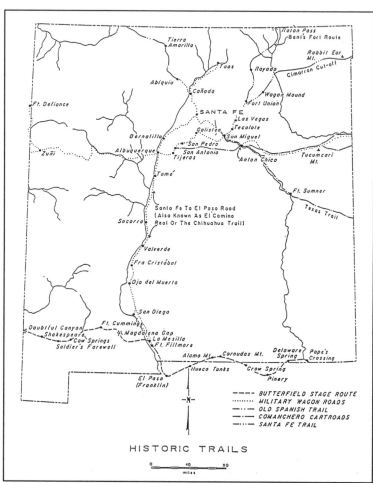

Reprinted by permission of University of Oklahoma Press

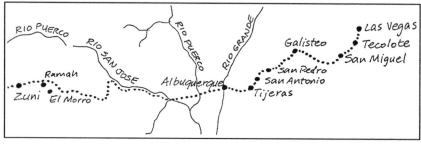

Likely route taken by the Millers on their flight west.

—1—

Flight from Fort Sumner

It was near midnight on July 14, 1881, when Sheriff Pat Garrett shot someone in Pete Maxwell's darkened bedroom in the old officers' quarters at Fort Sumner, New Mexico, where Maxwell lived. Sheriff Garrett said he had killed Billy the Kid, but when he was asked to sign an affidavit that it was the Kid he had shot, Garrett refused to sign. "I know who I shot", he said.

Garrett's deputies, Thomas McKinney and John Poe, were guarding the front porch that night when a young man brushed past them and backed into the house where he was shot by Garrett. McKinney and Poe accused Garrett of shooting the wrong man.

The next day a body was buried in the old Fort Sumner cemetery. Sheriff Garrett and a coroner's jury declared it was the body of Billy the Kid. But all through the years since that night, there have been doubts that it really was Billy the Kid's body they buried the next day.

On August 8, 1881, less than a month after the local newspapers reported the shooting death of Billy the Kid in Fort Sumner, New Mexico, at the hands of Sheriff Pat Garrett, a fair-haired young man who called himself John Miller and a petite, dark-eyed Mexican girl whose name was Isadora appeared before the parish priest, Father Berrera, and asked him to marry them. Young Miller was pale and weak, and white bandages covering a wound in his chest showed through his light summer shirt. A large caliber six-shooter hung from his hip.

Isadora later told friends and neighbors that some days before the shoot-out at Pete Maxwell's house the Kid had been wounded and she had taken him to her home in Fort Sumner. She tended his wounds and hid him between two straw mattresses, which she slid under the bed when officers came looking for him. When he was well enough to travel, the couple fled

Fort Sumner and headed towards the village of Las Vegas, where there were friends to help them.

The two young people who arrived in Las Vegas from Fort Sumner had adopted new identities along the way. Obviously fugitives from the law, they were hiding from view, traveling at night, and taking every precaution to throw anyone who might come looking for them off the track. So William Bonney became John Miller and was so known throughout the rest of his life.

Las Vegas in 1881 was a tough town, a town familiar with outlaws and killers. People in Las Vegas would have had no trouble spotting John Miller as a wounded outlaw on the run. Wherever he went he wore a pistol and kept a rifle within easy reach. And there was something else about Miller that would have attracted special attention: he looked like Billy the Kid. Since the Kid was known by sight to many people in Las Vegas, Miller took care to stay out of sight. The resurrection of the late gunfighter would have instantly become the chief topic of conversation. Talk like that had a way of spreading far and fast. In no time, it would have reached the ears of powerful people in the Territory who wanted to be sure Billy the Kid stayed conveniently dead.

The resemblance between John Miller and Billy the Kid was undeniable. Both had two prominent front teeth, slightly protruding. Both had piercing blue eyes, capped by heavy eyebrows (a characteristic of Billy's mother also). Both were of slight frame and medium height, with narrow sloping shoulders and slim hips. Both had small hands and large wrists. Because of this distinctive characteristic, Billy was several times able to free himself from handcuffs and escape from prison. Indeed, it was the method he had recently used to escape from the Lincoln County Courthouse fifteen days before he was to have been hanged. Miller liked to show off his ability to perform the same trick, asking friends to tie his wrists as tightly as possible. Then he would slip his hands free, laugh, and say: "Billy the Kid could do that."

Billy the Kid wore a black, high-crowned Mexican hat, dented on one side. Like the .41 caliber pistol he always wore on his hip, the black sombrero was a trademark of the Kid. John Miller wore the same style black Mexican hat, and was so attached to it that whenever he bought a new hat, he would sew the old Mexican brim onto the new crown. This eccentricity puzzled his friends for years.

At first meeting, one might mistake Miller for another fun-loving, carefree, twenty-one year old kid. But Miller had a dangerous temper, and when he was pushed too far, his blue-grey eyes turned steely hard and the skin under his eyes tightened almost to a squint. His body tensed, and no one could doubt that here was a man who would dare to shoot and aim to kill. Like Billy the Kid, John Miller was a wary man who always wore a loaded six-shooter. Miller was carrying an especially heavy load, a burden he was to bear for the rest of his life. He was a hunted man ever on the alert, ready to face death at any instant. The Santa Fe Ring, a powerful alliance of unscrupulous and treacherous men who were in almost complete control of the Territory of New Mexico, was after him. Miller knew if he ever let down his guard, he would be assassinated, or captured and hanged. Whenever people came unannounced to his door, day or night, through the years, they were startled to find Miller standing in the doorway with a loaded rifle aimed in their direction.

After the wedding, the twenty-one year old bridegroom and his young bride waited until after dark before setting out to continue their flight westward. Their friends in Fort Sumner and Las Vegas had equipped them for a long journey and for establishing a new home in rugged and inhospitable country. Isadora drove a fine team of horses, pulling a sturdy buckboard loaded with provisions. Miller rode a well-bred horse and drove seven head of cattle before the wagon. They were headed for the Mogollon Mountains in southwestern New Mexico, where some years earlier Billy the Kid had worked as a cowboy, and where his stepfather, William Antrim, was still residing. William Antrim, known to the inhabitants of the mining town of Mogollon as "Uncle Billy," never mentioned his step son, Billy the Kid. It is not known if Antrim's silence was due to an estrangement between himself and Billy. If so, it is strange that the Millers would have been heading for that particular place.

John and Isadora were alone in the world, hiding from the law, fleeing into the unknown. They slept beneath a tarp in the buckboard parked beside streams and the sluggish waters of the Rio Grande River, where their livestock could water and graze on the riverside foliage. Whenever they could, they parked their buckboard beneath hovering cottonwood trees that grew along the river banks and protected them from summer heat and from the curious eyes of travelers.

Miller and Isadora traveled the trails all through the night. At dawn they camped near water and trees if possible. During the day, the young man hid himself from view, while Isadora fed and watered the animals, milked the cows, and rested for the night's journey ahead.

Despite her small size, Isadora was tougher than one would suspect, which has caused speculation that she, too, may have had previous training in the skills of survival, possibly as Manuela, the wife of Charles Bowdre. Bowdre was a member of the Regulators, a group of young cowboys who rode with Billy the Kid during the Lincoln County War and who, after the war was over, earned a living rustling cattle and horses. Bowdre was killed by Pat Garrett's posse at Stinking Springs, where Billy was captured. Garrett's posse transported Bowdre's body to the Bowdre home in the old hospital building in Fort Sumner where Charles Bowdre, Manuela, William Bonney, who was also known as Billy the Kid, and several other cowboys lived.

Manuela arranged for Bowdre's burial in the Fort Sumner cemetery alongside his fellow Regulator, Tom O'Folliard. Shortly before, O'Folliard had been killed in front of the old hospital building when Pat Garrett's posse ambushed the Kid and the members of the Regulators as they rode into Fort Sumner to hide out at the Bowdre home.

After the death of her husband, it was rumored that Manuela turned her affections and loyalties to Billy the Kid, and lived with him thereafter.

There was, indeed, a striking resemblance between Isadora Miller and Manuela Bowdre. Both were Spanish speaking Mexican girls, dark-haired with flashing dark eyes and petite build, and both were cowgirls who could hold their own with the cowboys they rode with. It would have been a natural inclination for Manuela, who had shared the trials and the tragedies of the Regulators, to turn her attentions to Billy the Kid, who was the leader of the group and was himself in trouble. It is known that there was a close relationship between the Bowdres and Billy the Kid. For a time they were partners in a ranch near Portales, where they hid their stolen cattle and horses. When Sheriff Pat Garrett and his posse started trailing Billy, the Bowdres gave up the ranch and moved into the old abandoned hospital building in Fort Sumner, where the Kid and the Regulators often hid out when they came into town.

The 1880 census lists the Bowdre home as the official residence of William Bonney.

During their flight west, it is likely the Millers followed the military wagon roads, which had been charted by the United States Army to supply the military forts that had been established to control the Indians. The military roads linked the military installations with settlements along rivers and streams and through natural passes.

The Millers probably used the military road which connected Las Vegas with Fort Defiance on the far west border between New Mexico and Arizona. Leaving Las Vegas, this trail led to San Miguel, winding to Galisteo and then south to San Antonio and Tijeras and Albuquerque on the Rio Grande. It is likely the Millers chose to travel via a military trail because they knew that during summer rains, mud and mire would bog them down on a less traveled and rougher cattle trail. The cattle trail would have ensured more privacy from prying eyes, but would have made it impossible for a young man, weakened by wounds, and a young girl, slight of build, and no more than five feet tall, to extricate themselves and their equipment from a rain-soaked terrain. In making their tough choice, the Millers were forced to face the likelihood that they might be recognized by soldiers and travelers on the more heavily traveled military trail. However, if they could avoid detection, the military trail would lead them safely to their destination.

Miller knew that at any moment Thomas Catron, head of the infamous Santa Fe Ring, and Governor Lew Wallace, who had offered a reward for his capture, might learn that the shooting of Billy the Kid at Pete Maxwell's house had been faked. When the Millers left Fort Sumner, Garrett's deputies, McKinney and Poe, had been telling people that Garrett had shot the wrong man. To Miller's way of thinking, it would be only a short time before the truth would be out, and Catron's killers would come looking for him. So Miller was cautious; he wore his Mexican gaucho hat pulled down low over his ears to partially cover his face, and he traveled at night so he could not easily be recognized.

From Albuquerque the Millers traveled due west towards the Arizona border(see map). It was a long and hazardous trip under the best of circumstances, and the Millers were handicapped because they had to stay out of view as much as possible, and John Miller was weak from his wounds.

The Millers made their way as far as El Morro, famous even then for Inscription Rock, where earlier travelers, the Spanish Conquistadores, exploring the vast regions north of Mexico City, had stopped to water and feed their animals and to inscribe their names and messages in the soft sandstone. At Inscription Rock, the Millers, like the Conquistadores before them, found a place where they could water their animals in the year-round pond at the base of the rock, where their livestock could graze in nearby pasturelands, where they could build campfires to cook their meals, and where they could rest before setting out again in search of a safe haven in the wilderness.

After a short stay, the Millers left Inscription Rock and the military road, turned south, and according to some reports, made their way over mountains and rough trails to the mining town of Reserve, where they stayed until Miller had recovered from his wounds. Then they stopped for a while at the Nation's Ranch, a large cattle raising complex in the Quemado area, where John Miller obtained a job as a cook for a crew of Mexicans who were building a dam across an arroyo. Years later, Miller chose the Nation's Ranch as the spot to tell the story of Billy the Kid's escape from death in Fort Sumner and of his new life in another part of the Territory. He told the story to his young adopted son, Max Miller, a Navajo boy the Millers adopted when he was two years of age. Max Miller was interviewed in 1978 and told of his parents' escape from Fort Summer and their subsequent life in the Zuni Mountain area of New Mexico.

Max said that John Miller, whom he called "the Old Man," took him to the Nation's Ranch when he was a "little bitty feller". "There," Max said, "the Old Man told me the story of his escape from Fort Sumner to the Nation's Ranch, and told me to remember it."

Max did as he was told and memorized the story, just as his dad had told it to him, and here it is:

"My dad and mother were in trouble in Fort Sumner, and the Old Man was on the dodge, so they left Fort Sumner. They traveled only at night and my mother took care of the horses and milked the cows during the day, and the Old Man hid out. They went to Las Vegas. They arrived in Las Vegas on August 8, 1881,[1] thirty-one days after the Old Man was wounded in Fort Sumner and my mother took care of him, and hid him from the officers.

---

1. On August 8, 1881, thirty-one days after Miller's son Max said his Dad was wounded, the Millers arrived in Las Vegas. If Miller was wounded thirty-one days before August 8, it would indicate that Miller was wounded around July 8, some six days before Billy the Kid was supposed to have been shot by Garrett on July 14, 1881.

They changed their names and were married. They left Las Vegas and headed for the Mogollons, but when they came to the Nation's Ranch, they found a crew of workmen there building a dam across an arroyo. The Old Man got a job there as a cook and hired his team out to a Mexican. The Mexican was operating a dirt-moving slip. One day, the Mexican was whipping the Old Man's horses, and the Old Man went out and told him to stop. The Mexican tried to run over the Old Man with the slip.

"The Old Man said, 'He doesn't know who I am.' Then the Old Man went into the cookhouse and got his six-shooter. The Mexican ran into a shed, and the Old Man shot the shed full of holes until he ran out of bullets. The Mexican ran away, and my mother came out of the cookhouse and took the gun away from the Old Man.

"The Old Man said to me, 'This is where I fought my last battle.'"

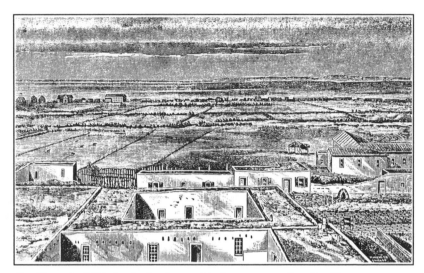

Las Vegas in 1880. In the background is the new town, East Las Vegas. (Wilson, 1880.) UNM Press

The Mogollon mountains, rich in minerals, beautiful, and deadly. Gold was discovered here in 1875. Its discoverer, Sgt. James Cooney, was killed by Apaches and is buried in a vault of rock near the town of Mogollon. (Sitgreaves, 1854.) UNM Press

This photograph of John Miller, which shows a remarkable resemblance to the only authenticated photograph of Billy the Kid, was probably taken when Miller was in his early 50's. This photograph is owned by Jewel Crockett Lambson who inherited it from her mother. The Crocketts owned a ranch adjacent to the Miller Ranch near Ramah, New Mexico. © 1989.

Charles Bowdre and wife. Courtesy Museum of New Mexico.

—2—

A Bloody Past

B illy the Kid's last battle is important not because it played any role in the larger drama of the Old West or the New Mexico frontier, but because it marked the true turning point in the life of the most famous of all the Western outlaws. No doubt Billy the Kid would have flushed his Mexican adversary from the shed at the Nation's Ranch and left another corpse lying in the New Mexico sand. John Miller was satisfied to cause some anxious moments for the careless man who had affronted him. The life of the gunslinger was over for Billy the Kid, the only life he had ever known.

Billy was born in New York, or maybe Illinois, Indiana, Kansas, or Missouri. No one really knows. Billy, however, using the name "William Bonney" in the 1880 census, claimed Missouri as his birthplace and stated it was also the birthplace of his parents. He was born Henry McCarty. At the close of the Civil War, his widowed mother, Catherine McCarty, was living in Indiana with her two sons, Joe and Henry. There she met William Antrim, a farmer and part-time bartender. At some point, the couple moved to Santa Fe, New Mexico, where they were married at the First Presbyterian Church in Santa Fe on March 1, 1873. According to records of the marriage, Mrs. McCarty's sons, Joseph and Henry, were in attendance. A later move took the Antrim family to Silver City, New Mexico, where, after a long bout with tuberculosis, Catherine McCarty died on September 16, 1874.

People who knew Henry in Silver City later recalled that he was a slender, almost delicate little boy who didn't seem to get into any more mischief than any other boy of that age and time. He did his chores and played with his friends when time allowed, but unlike many others his age, he never swore or got loud and rowdy.

During his Silver City years, Henry became fond of music and dance. He and a group of friends even formed a minstrel group that performed at the local opera house, with Henry in the role of "Head Man in the Show." The love of singing and dancing never left Henry Antrim. It stayed with him during the violent days when he came to be known to the world as Billy the Kid, and it remained during the long, desperate, anonymous years as an outlaw on the dodge named John Miller.

Within a year of his mother's death, young Henry Antrim had his first run-ins with the law. First, he was caught trying to sell stolen butter to a Silver City merchant. He was released after promising to mend his ways. But Henry had begun, for whatever reasons, his slide into living as he saw fit, whether that style of living fell within the bounds of the legal or not. Shortly after the butter incident, he began to associate with a local drunk and small-time thief named Sombrero Jack. One night, Sombrero Jack persuaded Henry to accompany him on a burglary of a Chinese laundry. The two made off with a bundle of clothing, but Henry was soon discovered with the goods by his landlady, who had him arrested.

Thinking to scare the boy out of his tendency for this sort of behavior, the sheriff locked Henry up in the town jail. But the boy persuaded the sheriff to let him have the run of the hallway outside his cell, and, left unguarded for half an hour, Henry climbed up the chimney and escaped. For the rest of his life, to one degree or another, Henry was to be on the run. And he had displayed for the first time the clever charm, the resourcefulness and the almost reckless daring that would mark his future career as outlaw and fugitive.

Henry Antrim now headed west, across the border into Arizona, where he remained for two years. He worked for a time at the Hooker Ranch, learning the skills of a ranch hand, handling horses and cattle, riding, roping, building barns, corrals and fences. He also learned to shoot, another vital skill on the frontier, and became proficient with both a rifle and pistol. It was here, too, that because of his youth, he acquired the name Kid Antrim, or more commonly just "the Kid."

But again, the Kid began to drift toward a life of crime. After being discharged from the Hooker Ranch, Henry took up with a small group of petty thieves and rustlers. Their primary occupation was stealing saddles and horses from the cavalry at Camp Grant and other Army posts. The details of the Kid's activities during this period are sketchy, but apparently he was arrested several times for horse theft, and each time managed to escape. He was proving a slippery man to keep confined. Then Kid Antrim's criminal ways took a more serious turn. In the little village of Bonito, Arizona, the Kid killed his first man, a blacksmith named Cahill, who was fond of bullying Henry and humiliating him in public. On the night of August 17, 1877, the Kid had as much as he could take, and he and Cahill got into a fight. Getting the short end of the proceedings with the bigger and stronger Cahill, the Kid pulled his six-shooter and shot Cahill in the stomach. Cahill died the next day. The Kid was quickly arrested and held in an Army guardhouse. But once again, before the wheels of frontier justice could grind further, the Kid managed to escape, steal a fast horse, and disappear. He headed east, back to New Mexico.

The boy who had fled Silver City to escape a charge of stealing laundry, returned to New Mexico a man fleeing an arrest warrant for murder, a man seasoned with two years surviving on the raw frontier of eastern Arizona, a man who could take care of himself. Henry Antrim returned an accomplished horseman and gunman. He could punch cattle, break horses, build a house, live in the backcountry, dodge Apaches and posses. And he could steal and kill if he needed to do so.

The Kid was a slim, wiry and tough young man, but also open, lighthearted, even charming. People liked him, and he liked people. He was never a loner. He still loved to dance and sing, and he had grown fond of the young Mexican señoritas of the little adobe villages, who, for their part, seemed quite taken with the boyish gringo and his laughing, merry-making way. Somehow he had learned to speak fluent Spanish, important not just for flirtations with dark-eyed señoritas, but also for making friends and allies in a part of the country still largely Hispanic.

But if a part of the Kid was still the sunny, fun-loving boy who took pleasure in singing at the Silver City Opera House, there was another side to him, a side that perhaps grew out of the life he was forced to live as an orphaned boy surrounded by hard and merciless men on the remote southwestern frontier. He had developed a hair temper, and as the fight with Cahill showed, a hair trigger as well. If provoked, he could explode in a violent rage. He was loyal to a fault, and believed strongly in sticking by his friends, no matter how despicable they might be. His light-heartedness easily crossed over into recklessness, so that if the impulse struck him, there was nothing too daring for him to attempt. The law held no particular sway over him. If it suited him to be law-abiding, he was. But he never let the law stand in the way of doing what he felt needed to be done.

It was at this time in his life that Billy the Kid became fascinated with guns. He practiced shooting his pistol whenever he could afford to buy ammunition. Marvelously dexterous with both hands, he became known as a two-gun shooter who could hit his target with either his right or his left hand and without seeming to take aim. He was very proud of his skill with a pistol and developed a repertoire of show-off tricks that he performed for admiring friends. Like the Apaches, he would sometimes shoot from a fast running horse, dodging behind the side of his horse to fire. Sometimes he would toss a hat into the air and shoot it full of holes before it fell, and at one time he trained a pet dog to stand still while he shot a ring around it. Billy's gun was a two-edged sword, one side for merry-making, the other for shooting first when the chips were down.

A few months after the shooting of Cahill, this pleasant young man with the quick trigger finger was in Seven Rivers, New Mexico. Soon William Bonney, as he now called himself, was working on the John Tunstall Ranch nearby and was about to become the leading figure in the bloodiest range war of them all, the Lincoln County War.

John Tunstall was an Englishman who had come to the New Mexico Territory to make his fortune. Tunstall had teamed up with local lawyer, Alexander McSween, to open a mercantile store in the little town of Lincoln, thus pitting the two partners against the long-time business power in the area, Major Lawrence G. Murphy. For a number of years, Murphy had run things as he saw fit in Lincoln County. The Sheriff, William Brady, was Murphy's man, and his business establishment, the so-called "House of Murphy," controlled Lincoln's mercantile and liquor business and also held the contract to supply beef to nearby Fort Stanton.

In this quartermaster enterprise, Murphy was allied with Thomas B. Catron, the most powerful man in the Territory and head of the notorious Santa Fe Ring. The Ring, a small group of business and political figures operating out of the Territorial capital of Santa Fe, controlled many facets of economic life in New Mexico. Most important, the Ring controlled the lucrative contracts to provision the Army posts and Indian agencies scattered throughout the Territory. The Santa Fe Ring was a ruthless operation, maintaining control of its far-flung empire through a shrewd blend of intimidation, corruption, bribery and violence. The Englishman John

Tunstall, perhaps unknowingly, had placed himself directly in the path of this band of thieves and killers. William Bonney knew nothing of all this. He liked his job as a cowhand on the Tunstall Ranch, he liked and respected his boss, and he liked the country. Before long, he made a close friend in a cowboy named Fred Waite, a part Chickasaw Indian from Oklahoma who was older and more educated than Billy. Inspired by the way in which the well-educated and gentlemanly Tunstall had made a success of his ranching endeavors, Billy and Fred Waite began to plan a similar path for themselves. They staked out a spread on the Rio Penasco, south of the Tunstall Ranch, and prepared to launch a farming and ranching operation of their own. But the clash between the Tunstall and McSween partnership and the House of Murphy soon erupted in violence that brought Billy's peaceful ranching days and the prospect of a respectable life to an end.

A band of Sheriff Brady's deputies came upon Tunstall on the trail between Lincoln and the Tunstall Ranch, in what is now called Tunstall Canyon, and gunned the Englishman down, claiming later that he had resisted arrest. Billy and three other Tunstall men heard the shooting from a hillside above the road. When the Sheriff's gang had left, the men rode down to find the body of their boss lying in the dusty road, shot through the head and chest.

Understandably, the killing of John Tunstall unleashed once again the darker side of Billy's nature. He was now bent on avenging Tunstall's murder. "I'll get some of them before I die," he told rancher Frank Coe. Since Sheriff Brady's men had done the killing, it was clear no justice could be expected from the local law enforcement element. So Billy joined a group of like-minded cowboys and gunmen who called themselves the Regulators. The Kid and a few other Regulators soon captured two members of the posse that had killed Tunstall. When these two deputies allegedly tried to escape, the Kid and his companions shot them to death. A month later, on April 1, 1878, Billy and the others struck back at the man they believed was the real murderer of Tunstall. From behind an adobe wall on the main street of Lincoln, the Regulators ambushed Sheriff Brady and a group of his deputies, killing the Sheriff and one of the deputies. The war was on.

The Territorial governor appointed one of Brady's deputies, George Peppin, the new Sheriff of Lincoln County. Convinced that Peppin was as bad as Brady, McSween obtained a warrant for Peppin's arrest from a sympathetic justice of the peace and assembled a force of some fifty men, among them Billy Bonney. On July 14, the McSween band rode into Lincoln. They surrounded the buildings housing the new Sheriff and his men, and a three day battle of occasional pot shots began. Finally, the influence of the Santa Fe Ring seems to have made itself felt. Colonel Dudley of Fort Stanton and a detachment of his troops arrived in town, claiming some of the troopers had been fired upon by the McSween crowd. Dudley positioned his men and his artillery piece such that even the most bellicose among the McSween force could see that the situation was hopeless. Two-thirds of the lawyer's army left during the night, leaving only McSween, his wife Susan, Billy and thirteen others, all holed up in the McSween house. The group held out for a day, but on the fifth day of the battle, deputies succeeded in setting the McSween house on fire.

In this desperate situation, the Kid took command and devised a plan of escape, something he was particularly good at doing. After dark, the McSween band dashed out of the flames and into darkness and gunfire. McSween and three others, including one of Peppin's deputies, died in the crossfire. The Kid and the rest escaped into the night.

Billy was a hunted man again, and he would remain a fugitive for the rest of his long life. He wrote Governor Lew Wallace protesting that he had only fought in the war to see justice done, and volunteering to tell in court all he knew about the trouble in Lincoln County. Wallace agreed to allow the Kid to testify and promised him an executive pardon for speaking out. Billy had a lot of friends in Lincoln County, and perhaps the promise of a pardon was Wallace's way of acknowledging the politics of the immediate situation. But the Lincoln County War was over and life gradually returned to a more normal pattern. People began to forget. So nothing came of the Governor's promise, and Billy grew more suspicious than ever of the authorities.

To earn a living, Billy joined former members of the Regulators, Charles Bowdre, Tom O'Folliard, and others who fought in the Lincoln County War, in a cattle rustling operation rounding up mavericks and range cattle and driving them across borders to sell. Billy and Charles Bowdre owned a "ranch" some seventy miles southeast of Fort Sumner at Los Portales where they hid the stolen cattle before they were sold.

To make matters worse for the Kid, a new Sheriff was now trailing him, an old acquaintance, a tough, determined lawman named Pat Garrett.

All through the late fall and early winter of 1880, Garrett relentlessly tracked Billy and his small band of outlaws across the rocky, snow-swept plains of eastern New Mexico. After several run-ins between the two, Garrett finally trailed the Kid to an abandoned rock house at a remote spot called Stinking Springs, about twenty-five miles east of Fort Sumner. Garrett's men surrounded the house in the dark of early dawn, and Garrett crawled close to get a closer rifle shot at Billy when he came out the door in the morning. But the wrong man was first out the door, and Garrett mistakenly shot Billy's friend, Charlie Bowdre. After a day of occasional gunfire, the outlaws decided there was no way to get past Garrett's men and offered to surrender. As Billy's gang filed out, Garrett's deputies searched and disarmed them. Then the Sheriff tied the outlaws tightly to their horses and led the ragged band of deputies and desperados to the Brazil ranch where Garrett obtained a wagon which he sent back to Stinking Springs to pick up the body of Charles Bowdre. Pat Garrett delivered the body to Bowdre's widow, Manuela, in the old hospital building in Fort Sumner where the Bowdres, Billy the Kid and other cowboys lived. It was Christmas Day.

Garrett took the outlaws to Las Vegas the next day, where a mob of angry citizens tried to seize one of the Kid's gang, Dave Rudabaugh, who was wanted for the brutal murder of a Las Vegas jailer. (Rudabaugh was a particularly nasty character. He later escaped from prison in Santa Fe and made his way to Mexico, where he terrorized a village until the peasants could endure it no longer. In a fury, they mobbed, beat and finally beheaded him.)

Garrett managed to get his prisoners safely on the train to Santa Fe, despite the shouts and threats Billy hurled at the lynch mob swirling about the train. Once securely in the Santa Fe jail, Billy again took up correspondence with Governor Lew Wallace, asking in several letters when the Governor intended to honor his promise of an executive pardon. In one of these correspondences, Billy reminded Wallace that he was in possession of letters dating back two years which certain parties were anxious to examine. The Governor ignored him, and no one has ever learned what these letters were.

On March 28, 1881, Billy was transported to Mesilla, New Mexico, some forty miles north of El Paso, to be tried there for the murder of Sheriff Brady. Judge Warren Bristol, a long-time associate of the Murphy crowd, sufficiently cowed the local Mexican jury, and on April 10, after two days of trial, the expected verdict came in. Bristol ordered Billy to be taken to Lincoln and on Friday the 13th of May to be hung by the neck until dead. Billy was held in the upstairs room of the Lincoln County Courthouse, which served as the jail. Since the room had no bars on the door or windows, Billy's ankles were firmly chained to the floor, and his wrists were handcuffed. Looking out the window, the Kid could watch workmen erecting his gallows. Besides Garrett, Billy was guarded by deputies "Pecos Bob" Olinger and J. W. Bell. Like the blacksmith Cahill some years before, Olinger was a big man who enjoyed tormenting the smaller Kid.

On April 28, Garrett was away on business. Olinger went across the street for a bite to eat and left the Kid in the charge of Bell. Billy asked for permission to go to the privy out back, and Bell accompanied him there. Inside, the Kid freed himself from the handcuffs and armed himself with a pistol apparently left there by a friend. Back in the courthouse, Billy pulled the gun and ordered Bell to put up his hands. But Bell struggled with Billy, knocked him down, then turned and started to run down the stairs. Billy shot him dead. "I did not want to kill Bell," the Kid later said, "but I had to do so to save my own life. It was a case of have to, not wanting to."

Finding Bob Olinger's shotgun in Garrett's office, the Kid climbed back up the stairs and positioned himself at the second story window overlooking the street, where he had a clear view of Olinger as he sprinted out of the Wortley Hotel. When Olinger was in range, almost directly below, Billy called out, "Hello, Bob," and when Olinger looked up, the Kid fired both barrels. Olinger died instantly. Billy borrowed a horse and rode out of town, still in chains.

After several months, Garrett received word that the Kid was not in Mexico, as almost everyone assumed, but hiding out in Fort Sumner at the house of an old friend, Pete Maxwell. Garrett and two deputies set out for Fort Sumner, arriving on the 14th of July.

The official story, as related by Pat Garrett, goes that the Sheriff went to the Maxwell house while Billy was at a dance. While the two deputies waited outside on the porch, Garrett questioned Maxwell in the bedroom. Suddenly, Billy appeared outside in the darkness, and, not recognizing the two men on the porch, drew his gun and asked, "Quien es? Quien es? Who is it?" Receiving no answer from the deputies, he backed into Maxwell's bedroom, asking "Pete, who are those fellows outside?" Only then did he see that Maxwell had a visitor. "Quien es?" he asked again, not wanting to shoot a friend. At this, Garrett pulled his gun, and still the Kid hesitated, not sure what was happening. Garrett fired twice, striking the Kid just above the heart on the first shot, killing him. Billy the Kid was buried the next day, July 15, 1881, in the Fort Sumner graveyard, between his old friends and fellow outlaws Charlie Bowdre and Tom O'Folliard.

But almost from the moment the shots rang out in Pete Maxwell's bedroom, doubts have been expressed about Garrett's version of events. For instance, many of those who knew the Kid said he would never have entered, let alone backed, into Maxwell's darkened bedroom after having been surprised by two strangers on the porch.

Some years later John Miller said: "Pat Garrett could not have shot the Kid in the chest. Garrett wasn't a good enough shot. He would have had to shoot the Kid in the back."

Doubts were fueled by the subsequent publication of Pat Garrett's own book, *The Authentic Life of Billy the Kid*, in which he wrote that his two deputies, McKinney and Poe, who were standing on the porch when the Kid entered Maxwell's house, accused him of shooting the wrong man.

Subsequently, there were many people who claimed they had seen Billy the Kid after he was supposedly shot by Pat Garrett.

Years afterward, there were warrants issued for the Kid's arrest.

In Las Vegas a poster dated March 24, 1882 (over six months after the shooting at Pete Maxwell's house), was circulated by a group of one hundred "Substantial Citizens" warning Billy the Kid and others if they were found within the limits of the city of Las Vegas after ten o'clock at night they would be invited to attend a "Grand Necktie Party."

The irregularities of the findings of a hastily recruited coroner's jury are well known. Three of the jurors were illiterate and each signed with an "X." One, Anton Sabedra, said afterwards that he had not viewed the body. Another, Sabal Gutierrez, was Pat Garrett's brother-in-law. The coroner's report was never officially filed, as required by law.

The body was hastily buried the morning after the killing. No clergymen were in attendance, and no one viewed the body except the immediate family members, Pat Garrett and his deputies, and supposedly, members of the coroner's jury.

Surely there was reason to wonder.

Navajo prisoners under guard constructing a building at Fort Sumner, New Mexico. Bosque Redondo circa 1864-68. UNM Press

Billy, Dave Rudabaugh, Billy Wilson, and Tom Pickett were captured on December 23, 1880, when they were hiding in a stone shack at Stinking Springs, near Fort Sumner. Garrett and his posse killed Charlie Bowdre and cut off the fugitives' food supplies until they surrendered. (Garrett, 1882.) UNM Press

Billy the Kid is killed by Sheriff Pat Garrett in Pete Maxwell's bedroom at Fort Sumner. (Garrett, 1882.) UNM Press

Best known picture of Billy the Kid. (Garrett, 1882.) UNM Press.

Pat Garrett had a controversial life. He was murdered in 1908. (Garrett, 1882.) UNM Press

Judge Warren Bristol came to New Mexico in 1872 from Minnesota to become a justice of the territorial supreme court. He presided at the trial of Billy the Kid in Mesilla. Bristol moved to Deming in 1885. (Haines, 1891.) UNM Press

Historic old jail and court house from which Billie the Kid made his last escape, Lincoln, New Mexico. Photo by Frasher. Courtesy Museum of New Mexico.

Pat Garrett was sheriff of Lincoln County after the Lincoln County War. Reportedly Garrett shot and killed Billy the Kid at Fort Sumner on July14, 1881.

Pete Maxwell House (officers quarters) Fort Sumner, New Mexico. circa 1885.
Courtesy Museum of New Mexico.

NOTICE!

TO THIEVES, THUGS, FAKIRS AND BUNKO-STEERERS,

Among Whom Are

J. J. HARLIN, alias "OFF WHEELER;" SAW DUST CHARLIE, WM. HEDGES, BILLY THE KID, Billy Mullin, Little Jack, The Cuter, Pock-Marked Kid, and about Twenty Others:

If Found within the Limits of this City after TEN O'CLOCK P. M., this Night, you will be Invited to attend a GRAND NECK-TIE PARTY,

The Expense of which will be borne by

100 Substantial Citizens.

Las Vegas, March 24th. 1882:

This poster was dated March 14th 1882—over six months after Billy the Kid was supposed to have been killed by Pat Garrett.

—3—

Building a New Life

After the shooting incident at the Nation's Ranch, the Millers knew it was too dangerous to stay there any longer. The couple packed up their few belongings and returned to El Morro. Soon, however, they were on the move again, headed further north and west, towards the Zuni Mountains, wild and remote country that promised the seclusion they sought.

As they made their way across the Zuni Indian lands, they met a man who was to play an important role in their attempt to build a new life, Jesus Eriacho, who was a powerful man in the western part of the Territory. Eriacho had been kidnapped as a child by Apaches from Arizona who used him as a slave. He was rescued by a Zuni man, Charlie Jesus, who hid him from the Apaches and raised him to manhood. A handsome, intelligent and ambitious man, over six feet tall with long flowing black hair, a dark mustache and surprisingly blue eyes and light skin, Jesus Eriacho commanded respect. When the Millers met him he was running a cattle herd on the open ranges in and around the Zuni Mountains.

Needing help over the coming winter, Eriacho made Miller a business proposition common among cattlemen in those days. If Miller would look after the herd on the Zuni range through the winter for the next five years, Eriacho would share with him the calves born in the spring. After five years, the herd would have doubled. Miller agreed, and in this way obtained a start for a herd of cattle of his own. It was the first of a number of deals with Eriacho. Over twenty years later, according to the records of McKinley County, New Mexico, Eriacho and Miller were still entering into business ventures.

That winter and for some time thereafter, John Miller lived alone in a shack he built inside a cave, and he tended Eriacho's cattle through the long months of snowstorms, bitter cold and occasional blizzards. Like all range cowboys, Miller was equipped with the necessities of survival. His pack horse was carefully loaded with provisions that would carry him through in spite of disasters, stampeding cattle and marauding animals. Miller's pack contained tarps and tents to protect him from the freezing cold of winter storms on the range, utensils for cooking, and survival foods consisting of corn, beef, jerky, and coffee. As the herd moved from one place to another in search of forage, Miller found shelter in various caves where he sometimes passed the lonely hours writing messages on the soft sandstone walls, which some people say are visible to this day.

Isadora stayed in an abandoned cabin nearby and delivered supplies to her husband on horseback. This arrangement not only kept Miller close to the herd he was responsible for, but also kept him out of sight of anyone who might come looking for him. Isadora brought not only food and clothing, but news of any suspicious characters poking around or asking questions.

The partnership between John Miller and Jesus Eriacho developed into a firm friendship. For a time the Millers and Eriacho even shared living quarters at the Norfleet Ranch, one of several ranches that had been purchased by Eriacho.

At some point in their early years in the Zuni country, the Millers found the spot where they would build a place of their own. The homesite they chose was on a hillside in a canyon, later known as "Miller Canyon," on a strip of land wedged between the Zuni and Navajo nations known as the Corridor. It was located several miles south of Ramah near the Mexican settlement at Atarke, and not far from Ojo Pescado. With the mountains behind them and meadows below, the Millers felt they had at last found a home. John Miller set about realizing his dream of a new life, a spread of his own where he could raise cattle, and sell and trade fine horses to neighboring Navajo and Zuni Indians and white settlers. Horses particularly were a life-long passion for Miller. All in all, Miller made a successful endeavor out of his dream. For over thirty years the Millers shared the hardships and triumphs of other early pioneers, shaping a new way of life in the wilderness. At Miller Canyon, Miller succeeded in putting the life of the gunfighter and outlaw permanently behind him.

When the Millers established their home at Miller Canyon they must have been very grateful to the Mormon missionaries who had been in the Ojo Pescado area before them and had established friendly relations with the neighboring Navajo Indians. Instead of hostile and bitter Indians, the Millers found a friendly Navajo Chieftain, Jose Pino, who had become a friend of the Mormon missionaries and was later baptized in the Church of Jesus Christ of the Latter Day Saints in the Mormon Temple in Salt Lake City.

Before the arrival of the missionaries, however, Jose Pino, a survivor of the Indian wars and of the notorious long walk to Fort Sumner, where he escaped from inhuman conditions, had controlled a band of Navajos. From time to time they raided the pueblo at Isleta and other settlements along the Rio Grande. There they stole sheep, women, and children from the Mexican settlers. They also waylaid the gold miners. The Indians were ignorant of the value of the greenbacks they stole, and E. A. Tietjen, one of the early Mormon explorers in the area, found them using the bills to roll their cigarettes.

In 1876, some five or six years before the Millers arrived at Pescado, Mormon missionaries were sent there by Brigham Young. One of the Mormon explorers of the Navajo-Zuni area, Anthony Ivins, a traveling missionary, had written the Mormon Church authorities from Ojo Pescado that it was a beautiful place, the land rich and the water good. "One hundred families might be sustained here," he wrote.

The following quotations were taken from the book *Encounter with the Frontier* by Gary Tietjen.

"In the year 1876 Brigham Young asked Lorenzo Hatch, to go to New Mexico and take charge of Indian work at Zuni. Hatch was joined by John Maughn and with their families they came to Ojo Pescado where they stopped a few weeks, then moved to San Lorenzo (now Tinaja), a Mexican village fifteen miles southeast of Ramah, where they spent the winter.

"In the same year Brigham Young wrote Ernest Tietjen and asked him to go on an Indian mission. He was asked to locate as near the heart of the Navajo Indian country as you can, learn their language, their habits, their customs and ways and teach them the gospel and a better way to live. . . .

"In November, 1876, Tietjen, accompanied by Luther C. Burnham, arrived in San Lorenzo. Brother Hatch located them in Savoya Valley, where Jose Pino, the Navajo Chieftain, pointed out the most favorable location.

"In June, 1882, a wagon train of Mormon converts from Arkansas were sent by Brigham Young to the Pescado area. They settled at Savoya some six miles above the present village of Ramah where they worked to convert the Indians to Mormonism, and to teach them a better way of life.

"The brave Mormon settlers at Savoya suffered a terrible first winter. One of the men had contracted smallpox as they were traveling through Albuquerque on their way to Pescado, and the whole colony was nearly wiped out. The Mormons remember with gratitude the kindness of the Navajo and Zuni Indians at that time who periodically left fresh meat just outside the colony, fearing to come closer, and the Zunis who even took some of the Mormon children into their homes to care for them until their parents recovered.

"After several years of food shortages, pestilence, and other hardships the colony of Savoya was temporarily abandoned because of the added danger of raiding Apaches, commandeered by Victorio."

How did John Miller, a twenty-two year old man, and his young bride, Isadora, survive in the wilderness near Pescado when the Mormon community was abandoned?

John Miller, often riding in luck, got a break when Victorio, who was responsible for driving the Mormons out of the area, was killed in October 1880, the year before the Millers arrived. That event more or less ended the Apache threat near Pescado. However, Geronimo was to go on the warpath in Southern Arizona and New Mexico several times after that until he was sent to Florida in 1886. Also, John Miller's skill with guns contributed greatly to his staying in the Ramah area in spite of Apache uprisings. In Lincoln County he had been next door to the Mescalero Apaches and they were frequently visited by the warlike Warm Springs band from across the Rio Grande, and so Miller knew a great deal about fighting Indians.

There is no doubt that John Miller was a skilled survivalist, who had learned how to live alone in the wilderness when he was still in his teens, before he became known as Billy the Kid. The years Billy worked as a cowboy in the Arizona and Western New Mexico mountains developed in him the skills of self-sufficiency which made him such a formidable foe during the Lincoln County War, and ensured his survival in the Zuni wilderness.

The life of a cowboy in the 1870's was hard, and soon made men of boys. There was no room on the range for weaklings. You learned to survive or you perished. Billy not only survived, but at an age when most young boys were attending school, Billy was learning how to bring down an antelope with a single shot, to keep a restless herd of longhorn steers from stampeding in a thunder storm, to cook over campfires and in fire pits, to construct shelters from materials at hand, and to look death in the face with a cool and calculating eye.

Also, John Miller was lucky. His relationship with the Zuni rancher, Jesus Eriacho, was a big factor in helping him to establish himself as a respected cattleman and horse-trader in the Zuni Mountains, where he was accepted as a friend by the Zuni and Navajo inhabitants. Where others might perish, John Miller, alias Billy the Kid, would survive.

When the Millers arrived at Pescado, only one Mormon missionary remained in the area. He was Ernest Tietjen, who had stayed behind when Brigham Young called the other Mormons back to Utah. Tietjen's purpose was to convert the Indians to Mormonism and to continue work on a reservoir he was building at Ramah. He accomplished the reservoir project with a scraper made with scraps from Fort Wingate and one yoke of oxen. Tietjen also owned a little flour mill which he operated with one horse. The mill provided graham flour, sometimes diluted with sunflower seeds. Wheat was often threshed in the Zuni fashion. A round flagstone courtyard served as the threshing floor. Horses were driven around and around in the enclosure, threshing the grain with their hooves.

"The ingenious Ernest Tietjen also had a hand turned mill he had made of oak, which was like a wringer on a washing machine. He grew a variety of hardy sugar cane and wrung out the sap with the wringer, and boiled it down into a molasses candy. He evaporated milk by freezing it and removing the frozen water and he had rigged up a Dutch mill which turned another wheel with buckets on it. The buckets pulled water out of a dammed up arroyo for watering the garden".(*Encounter with the Frontier* by Gary Tietjen).

John and Isadora Miller must have been especially grateful for the flour mill operated by Ernest Tietjen when he was the only other white man around, and the only flour available was the stone-ground flour the Indians made by grinding corn in a hollowed rock (metate), with a rock held in the hand (mano). The resulting product had a devastating effect on the teeth of all who consumed it.

Miller built his house on the hillside in Miller Canyon with his own hands from trees he felled and hewed into logs for the outside structure and lumber for floors and doors, topped with a tin roof that shone in the sun, and kept out the rain.

The log house with the tin roof and large iron woodburning stoves was a great comfort to Isadora and John Miller who, for several years had lived in caves and abandoned cabins. At last they were comfortable and secure. When angry mountain storms beat a crescendo on the tin roof, they huddled close beside the iron stove while the big room filled with the scent of burning pine, cedar, and pinon logs, cut from an endless forest of firewood just outside their back door.

Feliz Bustamante, who lived with the Millers for a year when she was a little girl, said the Miller home was built in the familiar "L" shape consisting of one long room and a smaller side room. The large room was furnished with two handmade beds, tables, chairs, and storage chests. In the center of the room was a large woodburning stove which heated the room. It also served to keep water hot in a big kettle which sat on top of the stove and which Miller used to brew endless pots of coffee. Several pistols were hung on the wall, and a loaded rifle always stood in the corner by the door. The kitchen was furnished with a two-lid wood burning stove, shelves made from wooden boxes, and a hand hewn table and chairs.

Austere as it was, the Millers lived there for over thirty years, adding out-buildings and corrals to house and care for the livestock and equipment they accumulated through the years.

In the courtyard behind the house John Miller hand-dug a well, lined it with cedar logs, and built a windmill and water tank to furnish water for the household and for the animals.

Through the years, Miller added four or five rooms to the main house, which he built like a fort, with no windows and no connecting doors. Miller used the rooms to house various people who stayed at the Miller Place, including the outlaws he rode with after the Lincoln County War who came by and kept him informed as to the machinations of Thomas Catron and his hired killers in the Santa Fe Ring, and warned Miller of Catron's efforts to trace him.

John Miller had no fear of the friendly Navajo and Zuni Indians who inhabited the area when he arrived, nor of the Mormon pioneers who soon returned to establish a permanent settlement at nearby Ramah. John Miller was haunted then, and for the rest of his life, by the specter of the hangman's noose that had almost claimed his life in Lincoln. His goal was to avoid Thomas Catron and his cohorts in the Santa Fe Ring who exerted ominous influence over the affairs of the Territory, and wanted to see Miller dead. Miller was sure they were looking for him all over the Territory, and he knew they might show up at any time in an attempt to ambush him. So, day and night, Miller was always on guard with a loaded pistol on his hip, and a rifle nearby, relying upon his ability to shoot first. Miller had no illusions about the intent of the authorities in Santa Fe, and was not willing to risk again the promise of a pardon. Miller was determined that he would not be taken alive.

Although Miller was cautious, he never became a recluse. As wild as the mustangs he rode, and as hard to tame, Miller showed up everywhere anything was going on. He was a frequent participant in community affairs in the Navajo and Zuni Indian villages, at dances in the Mormon community, at spring and summer roundups, and was often seen at trading posts throughout the area, where he mingled with other cowmen and outlaws who were passing through.

In spite of Miller's vows to himself and to others that he would stay out of trouble, Miller might not have made it without the help and devotion of his wife, Isadora. It was Isadora, steadfast and patient, who kept the home fires burning. It was she who ministered to the sick, tended the gardens, fed and watered the animals and cared for their little Navajo son when a restless Miller was roaming the countryside.

When the 1900 Census for Valencia County, Jaralozo Precinct #24 was recorded, John Miller, his wife, Isadora, and a young man by the name of John Hill were living in the house at Miller Canyon. John Miller listed his occupation as a stock raiser, his birthdate as 1857, and his age as forty-two. His birthplace was recorded as Texas, and the birthplace of his parents as Kentucky. Isadora listed her birthdate as 1849, her age as fifty, and her birthplace and the birthplace of her parents as New Mexico. John Hill listed his age as twenty-two, and his occupation as stock-herder. For reasons unknown, Max Miller, adopted son of the Millers, was not listed in the 1900 census.

It is evident that John Miller had established himself as a respectable rancher in the community, and was hiring help to work with his growing herds of cattle and the breeding and training of his fine horses.

Ten years later, the 1910 census listed the Miller Place in McKinley County, Precinct #4, Ramah. John Miller and Isadora, for reasons of their own, had changed both his and Isadora's ages, listing both as age fifty-eight. The 1910 census also recorded the addition of a son, Max, age sixteen, living at the Miller home.

It was Miller's usual practice to change his age and birthdate on all official records. One can speculate that this was just another method he used to throw authorities who might be looking for him off the track.

This picture of John Miller at the Miller Ranch with one of his fine cow horses, was probably taken when Miller was in his 40's. For the first time Miller is shown smoking a pipe, and for the first time he is shown without a gun holster. His gun is tucked under his belt. This photograph is owned by Jewel Crockett Lambson who inherited it from her mother. © 1989.

Gary Lane Tietjen is a writer and historian who wrote extensively about the Ramah-Zuni area and the Mormon pioneers who lived there, in his book "Encounter with the Frontier". Tietjen lives in Los Alamos where he is employed.

Jesus Eriacho was a rancher, cattleman and Governor of the Zuni Pueblo. He was also a friend and business partner of John Miller. This picture was taken when Eriacho and other ranchers were in Springerville, Arizona, at the trial of horse thieves who had raided their ranches. Photo Courtesy of Chimeco Eriacho.

—4—

Billy's Friend Herman Tecklenburg

At some point after his flight west, John Miller met a friend, Herman Tecklenburg, a man he had known during his outlaw days in Fort Sumner and Oklahoma. Tecklenburg had followed the cattlemen and miners to the western part of the state of New Mexico. When he met up again with John Miller, Tecklenburg was an Indian scout stationed at Fort Wingate near Bear Springs. Herman Tecklenburg had known John Miller when Tecklenburg was working as a cowpuncher around Fort Sumner and Miller was an outlaw known as Billy the Kid, who was dodging Pat Garrett and his posse. Thereafter, around the Ramah area where Tecklenburg and Miller both lived for many years, Tecklenburg was known to be John Miller's most trusted friend.

Tecklenburg told many people in the area that he knew John Miller was Billy the Kid. Tecklenburg's son, John Herman Tecklenburg,[2] remembers John Miller visiting with his father at their home near McGaffey. The two old friends, John Miller and Herman Tecklenburg, sat up most of the night on an outside log, telling stories about the Old Days when Herman Tecklenburg was a young immigrant from Germany looking for adventure in the Wild West, and John Miller was a young gunslinger fighting the Lincoln County War.

Herman Tecklenburg was born in Schwarme, Hannover, Prussia, in 1865. When he was about eleven years of age his father, fearing that war was coming, urged his son to go to America where he would be safe. Young Tecklenburg could not obtain papers for emigration, so he stole aboard the *S.S. Nuremburg* by tagging along with several women emigrants and their

---

2. John Herman Teckleburg, the son of Herman Tecklenburg, died in 1989, at the age of ninety. John Herman Tecklenburg was interviewed for this story about his Dad and John Miller in 1989 at his home in Los Lunas, New Mexico, where he lived with his wife, Nora.

children. When he was discovered by the ship's crew, he was made to work as a steward to pay for his passage.

Tecklenburg worked for a while in a grocery store in Hoboken, N.J. for $5 per month plus his keep, but he was enamored of the Wild West, and he soon journeyed westward by working as a cowpuncher and coal miner and met up with Billy the Kid along the way. Young Tecklenburg was six years younger than Billy. A boy early in his teens, he must have reminded the Kid of his own early transition from childhood to manhood.

Herman Tecklenburg never saw any member of his family in Germany again, but he lived a long and exciting life on the Western Frontier. Tecklenburg punched cattle, drove the mule freights, worked as an Indian Scout for the U.S. Army and farmed up near McGaffey at the Boone Ranch in McKinley County, New Mexico, where John Miller, alias Billy the Kid came to visit him.

"Sometimes," Tecklenburg said, "I saw more of the Wild West than I had bargained for."

In an interview for the *Gallup Independent* of August 9, 1944, Herman Tecklenburg talked to columnist Wesley Huff about his life as a frontiersman and about his long friendship with John Miller:

"They shot somebody over at Fort Sumner," Tecklenburg said, "and they buried him there and put an end to the hunt for Billy the Kid. But it wasn't Billy they shot. Billy and his Mexican wife escaped over into Old Mexico, and when I was living at Page (near McGaffey) about thirty-five years ago, he came with Lou Shoemaker to visit me and we talked over old times. He was ranching it down near Ramah. They all knew of him down there as Billy the Kid, but never spoke of it for fear of getting him in trouble. He was a prince. The big shots made him out to be an outlaw because they couldn't handle him. Down at Ramah he was known as John Miller."

Herman Tecklenburg said it was in his cow-punching days that he knew Billy the Kid in Fort Sumner. "The Kid had many friends there," he said, "and resentment ran high when outsiders came there to hunt the outlaw, for they knew him as a friend.

"Billy the Kid would kill and butcher a maverick and ride all night leaving cuts of it with the poor people so they could eat," Tecklenburg said. "That's how bad Billy the Kid was. He was no cattle thief.

"All they have to do is say something bad about Billy, and I see red. I knew him as a friend, and he was no cow thief or bad man.

"Thirty-five years ago we lived on the old Boone Place under the hill at Page. Billy the Kid and Lou Shoemaker came to the house there and stayed with me overnight. We traded horses and talked over old times. The Kid was no dead man. He and his wife were living on their ranch over near Ramah and went by the name of John Miller.

"He was a prince. Them was the kind of men who made the West. They did the fighting to bring civilization, not the business people in the towns. They didn't know what was going on."

Ginger Moody is the great-granddaughter of the frontiersman, Herman Techlenburg.

Herman Tecklenburg was a fabulous frontiersman who rode with Billy the Kid and the Regulators when he was barely fourteen years of age. Later Tecklenburg was an Indian Scout, mule driver, cowpuncher and Rancher who lived in the Ramah-Zuni mountain area where he met up again with Billy the Kid (alias John Miller.) Photo courtesy of Ginger Moody, 1990.

John Herman Tecklenburg was the son of Herman Tecklenburg, the frontiersman who was a pal of Billy the Kid, and who later was a neighbor of John Miller in the Zuni Mountain area. This picture was taken at John Herman Tecklenburg's home in Los Lunas when he was interviewed in 1988, a few months before his death.

—5—

Apollas Boaz Lambson

One of the early Mormon settlers in the Ramah area was Apollas Boaz Lambson, a trader and businessman, who became a good friend of John Miller and his wife, Isadora, and had numerous business dealings with them. Apollas Lambson moved to the Ramah area in 1891 with his wife and thirteen children.

Shortly thereafter, Lambson's wife, Angenette Permelia, was operated on for a tumor. A resulting infection caused her death shortly thereafter during childbirth. The newborn baby, her fourteenth child, also died. Mother and baby were buried by her eldest son beneath a concrete slab. Many years later, her husband Apollas Lambson was buried there also. The twelve Lambson children who were still at home after the death of their mother, were raised by their father under extremely difficult circumstances.

Frontier people built their log cabins and learned to help one another survive. It would not have occurred to a frontiersman to call upon a distant government to help in times of need. Indeed, a civil servant of those days would have thought him insane for asking. Governments were for maintaining law and order and sometimes even that was impossible on the frontier. Apollas Lambson and his family survived with courage, hard work, and ingenuity, as did the other Mormon settlers and people like John and Isadora Miller. They all knew what was expected of them, and they asked no quarter. By their own efforts they established a new generation of hardy people on the frontier, and helped to build a new country that became the envy of the world.

Apollas's son, Eugene Lambson,[3] second youngest in the family of thirteen children, was born in 1888, and was three years of age when the family moved to Ramah. Eugene Lambson was interviewed in July, 1976, when he was eighty-eight years of age.

---

3. Eugene Lambson died in 1979.

During his long life on the Western Frontier, Eugene Lambson was an active participant in everything that was going on. He worked in logging camps. He was a cook, a wrangler, an Indian trader, a farmer, missionary, musician, sheepherder, Director of the Indian Ceremonial Association in Gallup, a restaurant owner, and a movie actor.

Some of the movies Eugene Lambson appeared in were:

The Texas Ranger with Jack Oakie.

New Mexico with Errol Flynn and Jane Wyman.

Red Mountain with Alan Ladd and Elizabeth Scott (Eugene doubled for Ladd in the riding scenes.)

Big Carnival with Kirk Douglas and Jan Sterling. (Eugene was contact man for this movie.)

Arrowhead with Charlton Heston and Mary Sinclair. (Eugene said this was the first movie Heston ever made.)

Eugene Lambson recalled the difficult years when he and his brothers and sisters were growing up in the Ramah area. "It was especially hard when sickness befell the family," he said. "I remember one terrible time when my brother Frank, Dad, and I were visiting our brother, Orva, who was working in a mine in Clifton, Arizona. We were all staying in a one-room house, all six of us, and we all came down with smallpox, and we were quarantined. The doctor, Dr. Horn, told us to stay there until we were over it. We got tired of that, and went fishing for a week on the Blue Canyon, and ran into Dr. Horn there. He told us to get back to the house fast, and we got back there fast."

Another time Lambson said he and his Dad and brother Frank were on a trip to Prescott, Arizona, and came down with diphtheria, and were quarantined and recuperated in their wagon. "But we had learned to batch it pretty good," Lambson said, "and we survived."

Eugene said that when he was about six years of age, "my Daddy started a little Indian trading post and went to buying sheep and goats, and traded with the Navajos. I went to herding sheep and goats. I was six years old, and I got no education at all. So I herded sheep and goats until I was about nine years old."

There was one particularly bad time when Lambson was about nine years of age when he and a Navajo lad were sent out on the range to herd goats. "The only food we had were roasted prairie dogs," he said.

When Eugene Lambson was old enough to work outside the home, he was employed by the Englishmen, Giles and Bob Master, at the Master

Brothers Trading Post, the first trading post in the village of Ramah. Eugene recalls that John Miller and friends from the Mexican communities south of Ramah often came into Ramah to trade with the Master brothers for supplies they needed at home.

When Eugene Lambson was asked if he thought John Miller was Billy the Kid. He answered positively: "I know he was."

And then Lambson elaborated: "It was generally understood up around Ramah that John Miller was a fugitive, and most people thought he was Billy the Kid. Herman Tecklenburg, for instance, was a good friend of John Miller and he told us for sure that he knew that John Miller was Billy the Kid. Herman Tecklenburg was an early settler, and owned a ranch up in the Zuni Mountains. Then there was the Crockett family, whose land adjoined the Miller land. All of the Crocketts will tell you that they knew that John Miller was the Kid.

"My father and John Miller were good friends," Lambson said. "Even though we knew John Miller was a fugitive from justice, we remained friends because he tended to his business and we tended to ours, and he was a good neighbor.

"In the early years," Lambson continued, "we probably heard more about John Miller than most people because my sister, Hesseltine Lambson, was dating one John Hill who lived at the Miller Place. Hill said John Miller talked a lot about Billy the Kid, but never admitted that he was the Kid. John Hill had a beautiful singing voice, and John Miller could sing pretty good, too, and they liked to harmonize, especially cowboy songs. John Hill never married. Later he moved to Los Lunas where he ran a service station for many years.

"John Miller liked to dance, too, and often attended the dances in Ramah where I played the fiddle for community dances, sometimes in the living room of my house. Miller was a good dancer and all of the girls were pleased when he showed up at the dances and asked them to dance."

Eugene Lambson recalled visiting the Miller home when he was a young boy. "Dad sometimes bought horses from John Miller, and sold some to him. One time Dad sent me and my brother Frank over to the Miller place to pick up a horse he had bought.

"When we rode up to the Miller Place on our horses, the dogs started barking, and John Miller came out the door of the house with a 30-30 rifle pointed at us. We were really scared, but he soon recognized us. You're the Lambson boys, aren't you? he asked.

"We replied that we were, and he told us to dismount, unsaddle our horses and feed them. He said we were to stay there that night because it was late, and we lived about fifteen miles from the Miller place.

"I'll always remember that night," Lambson reminisced. "We didn't go to bed at all. John Miller made pot after pot of coffee all night long. I'll bet he drank fifteen or twenty cups, and told us stories about Billy the Kid and gunfighters. He said he had been in a lot of gunfights, and showed us seven scars on his legs where he had been shot."

Unfortunately, Eugene Lambson could not remember details of the gunfighter stories John Miller told. The stories had faded from his memory and had been lost in the mists of time.

Lambson remembered, however, that John Miller was always armed. "If he wasn't wearing his pistol, which he wore most of the time, he had a rifle nearby. That's one way we knew he was a fugitive from justice," Lambson said. "He was always ready to shoot anyone who came to take him in."

Lambson recalled that John Miller was alone in the house the night the Lambson boys were his guests. "Miller told us his wife, Isadora, and his son Max had gone to El Paso for supplies," Lambson said.

In spite of close questioning, Lambson insisted his memory was accurate when he said Isadora Miller and her young son often drove a team of horses pulling a wagon from Ramah to El Paso more than three hundred miles over rough cattle trails, through territory where people were terrorized by bandits and outlaws and unfriendly Indians of the dread Apache Tribe.

Lambson did not appear to think that the trip to El Paso was anything unusual. "They went at least once a year," he said, "and sometimes John Miller went with them. They always traveled at night, and when Miller went with them, he left the farm and livestock in care of John Hill."

One can only speculate why John and Isadora would brave the dangers of the long trip to El Paso. Perhaps Isadora was lonely for friends and family who lived across the Rio Grande in Mexico, and went to visit them. Or she may have gone for the purpose the Millers claimed. She made the long trip to stock up on supplies. Lambson's account of the Millers' trips to El Paso would tend to corroborate the reports of people in the El Paso area who insist they saw Billy the Kid there years after he was supposed to have been killed by Pat Garrett at Fort Sumner.

Lambson remembers another evening he spent with the Millers at their cabin when Isadora invited him to have dinner with the family. Lambson remembered he was served hot tortillas which Isadora made by forming a soft dough, patting the tortilla flat on her knee and tossing it on the stove lids to cook. "With frijoles and chili, it wasn't bad at all," he said.

Eugene Lambson volunteered an unusual story concerning his Dad, Apollas Lambson, and Pat Garrett: "My father," Lambson said, "was a friend of Pat Garrett when Garrett was stationed at Holbrook, Arizona, and my father was living seven miles south of the town and was selling salt to the Mormon settlers. Pat Garrett told my father about the night he was supposed to have shot the Kid at Fort Sumner."

Lambson's report of the shooting of the Kid by Pat Garrett differed somewhat from the usual accounts of that event. Lambson's version goes like this: "Pat Garrett, in the company of his deputies McKinney and Poe, learned that the Kid was in Fort Sumner, holed up at the house of Pete Maxwell. They sneaked up to the house in the dead of night, and Garrett knocked on the door. A Mexican youth with a gun in his hand answered the knock and queried: "Quien es?" Sheriff Garrett pushed the door open and fired. The Mexican youth fell dead, and Garrett told the Kid and his girl who was there with him, to pack up and leave Lincoln County forever."

Lambson said that Garrett deliberately allowed the Kid to escape because "Garrett and the Kid were friends. Garrett didn't want to kill the Kid, and had been dragging his feet about bringing him in. But because of the killing of two guards when the Kid escaped from the Lincoln jail, the pressure was on the sheriff to do something."

It is an interesting speculation to suppose that the Millers may have visited Pat Garrett and his family who were living in the El Paso area when the Millers made their yearly trips to El Paso for supplies.

Eugene Lambson, like the Millers, was grateful for the support of the Navajo Chieftain, Jose Pino, during the early years. This report was written about Eugene Lambson and Jose Pino, whom Lambson called Old Man Many Beads, and the buckskin rope that was given to Eugene when Old Man Many Beads died:

"Old Man Many Beads, who was named Jose Pino by the Mexicans, was born on the Navajo Reservation, and came to the Ramah Area about age seventeen. His corn field and hogan were in back of the present Ramah Trading Post. He was a great hunter and tanned hides and had buckskins, so he hired two Navajos from the Reservation to come braid the twelve-strand buckskin rope and gave them a horse apiece. This was about 1862.

"When the Navajos from Ramah were taken to Fort Sumner in 1864, Many Beads was there only about a year when he, his wife, and another Navajo escaped and came back to Ramah, bringing the rope with them. Since there were no Indians here, they went on to the Mescalero Apache people. His son Petogal was born while there. When the Navajos were turned loose from Fort Sumner, Many Beads felt free to come back to Ramah, bringing his wife, baby and the buckskin rope.

"All through his life, Many Beads used this rope for roping stock. When he died about 1919, he was buried by Gene Lambson and Jess Johnston in an allotment in a Ramah Canyon called Tsa'co. They made a rough box and took it up the Canyon, dug a grave, went down to the hogan to get the body where it was lying on a sheepskin. They took Many Beads and rolled him up in a blanket and put him in a pickup, along with all of his worldly belongings, saddle, bridle, blanket, beads and moccasins. This all went into the coffin with Many Beads.

"After Petogal watched his father being buried, he took the buckskin rope which had not been placed in the coffin; caught the black horse which had been a pet saddle horse for the old man for many years, led the horse up to within thirty yards of the grave and shot the horse with a .22 rifle so Old Man Many Beads could have him to ride for ever after. Through a superstitious idea, he said, 'Don't you ever let a Navajo have this rope.' And he gave it to Gene Lambson as the last of his father's possessions."

Eugene Lambson always kept the rope hanging on the back of his front door. It is now owned by Eugene's daughter, Daisy Boyd.

Max Miller told Robert (Swede) Lambson that he called Jose Pino "Grandpa."

Jose Pino knew that John Miller was Billy the Kid. Pino was one of the few people Miller trusted to keep his secret.

The Lambson family left Ramah in 1935. However, Eugene Lambson returned in 1945 and opened a malt and sandwich shop in the village, because he was not ready for retirement, and he liked the comfortable old house just off the main street of Ramah, where he lived for the rest of his life. "It is the oldest house in Ramah," he said. "I can remember in the old days, I played the fiddle and we held square-dances in the living room."

Apollas Boaz Lambson and wife, Angenette Permelia: Apollas Lambson was an early business man and trader in the Ramah-Zuni area who was a friend and business associate of John Miller and who also knew Pat Garrett. Lambson was convinced that Miller was Billy the Kid. Photo courtesy of Jewel Lambson, 1990.

Eugene Lambson, wife Sarah, and son Robert.
Eugene Lambson was a business man and trader in the Ramah
area who had many business dealings with John Miller.
Photo courtesy of Jewel Lambson, 1990.

—6—

The Mormons Return

In June, 1882, with the breakup of the Mormon colony at Sunset, Arizona, another ten families settled at the present site of Ramah.

Unlike other pioneers who came to the western frontier individually, hoping to survive by their own ingenuity and capabilities, the Mormons came as an integrated community. The men were handpicked to meet most of the community needs for skilled manpower: there was a carpenter, a blacksmith, a tanner, a stone mason, a midwife, and wherever possible, a teacher. Nevertheless, the early Mormon settlers experienced almost unbelievable hardships.

Historian Gary Tietjen writes the following in his book, *Encounter with the Frontier:*

"Annie Burke recalls that the settlers were given 24 lbs. of flour, 4 lbs. of sugar, and 5 lbs. of grease to last all winter. The Bond family she says, had a yoke of oxen and an old milk cow they had been given in Sunset. The old cow gave a quart of milk a day and no cream. That was the extent of their groceries. Before winter set in they ate red roots, pigweeds, dandelions, sourdock for greens and lamb's quarter. Salt, pepper, and vinegar served as seasoning. Occasionally they found a few sage lilies and put them in their milk gravy. Earnest Tietjen's third wife, an Indian, taught the settlers to search for wild onions and wild potatoes to sustain life. A little parched corn kept many a family alive when there was little else to be had. Whatever was to be eaten in the winter had to be gathered in by fall.

"Mary George McNeil tells of an incident which happened while they were living near Savoya: 'Sometimes the winter hung on too long. Once when there was no food left but one loaf of bread, Father gathered us all around and asked us if we were willing to save that one loaf for the baby. We all said we were. He went out then and managed to find and kill a porcupine. We cooked it all one day and couldn't eat it. . . it was so tough. So we cooked it another whole day and it would still pull your teeth out to try and eat it. After we ate the porcupine, he found some prickly pears. . . just as knotty and sticky as could be. We ate those. Finally Grandpa Pipkin from up the canyon sent word that he had some flour to loan Father, so Father went over the mountain to get it. He was so weak he could hardly get back in the snow, but he told me that he would think of his children starving and that would keep him going.'

"By 1883 the Mormon settlers in Ramah had begun the process of establishing a permanent community there. A one-room (12x18) meeting house was built which served as church and school, and the residents were busily building their own homes and businesses.

"Education was not to be neglected. Parents paid the teacher so much for each child sent to school. Phoebe McNeil was enlisted to teach, but some of the children had to tend her baby while the others recited. Children brought their own benches and Mrs. Clawson still remembers with envy the beautiful bench possessed by one of the Garn children. Slates were used to write on. If a slate were broken accidentally, the pieces were carefully saved for writing material.

"In those early days the Rahmans went to Wingate for most of their supplies. Mail came once a week, by horseback, from Wingate. Gallup was nothing more than the coal mine and the Black Diamond Store.

"In 1886 some of the Church's General Authorities visited Ramah and asked that the streets be straightened and aligned with the cardinal directions. This was an important matter, and at least one of the cabins had to be torn down to comply with the request. Beautification of the town was urged. Naturally the settlers had been instructed to make wide streets. Lombardy poplars, imported from Italy to Utah, thence to Ramah, gave the town the traditional mark of Mormon settlement.

"Milk was kept in the cellars. The settlers raised rutabagas, beets, potatoes, wheat, and corn, but nothing was known about preserving food. Meat could be kept for long stretches of time in cold weather by hanging it on the north side of the house. As the weather warmed up, the meat would be wrapped in a heavy tarp in the daytime and hung out at night. Of course the root vegetables could be kept fairly well in damp sand in the cellars. Dick

Bloomfield later built an icehouse. In the winter the ice was stored in layers of sawdust and provided the community with ice throughout the summer.

"There were no doctors in Ramah, and no medicines to be had. The midwives were skillful in the use of herbs and nursing, however, and very seldom lost a patient."

One of the early Morman pioneers in Ramah was William Bond who, with his wife Elvie, owned a ranch above the village of Ramah and across the mountain from the ranch owned by Herman Tecklenburg. William Bond's son, Atheling Bond, at the age of twenty-three established a trading post in Ramah which traded goods and food supplies with the surrounding Navajo and Zuni Indians and the white settlers.

Atheling Bond was interviewed in 1978, when he was eighty-nine years of age, at his home on Main street, not half a block down the street from the Bond Trading Post, which he had operated throughout his life, and which is now owned by his son, Edgar.

Atheling Bond was successful in the many business endeavors in which he was engaged, and was an important and respected man in the community of Ramah and throughout McKinley County. As a member of the Mormon Church, he was a leader in church affairs, and a faithful member of the church all of his life. The beautiful Ramah Chapel of the Church of Jesus Christ of Latter Day Saints (Mormon) which Atheling Bond helped build, dominates the village of Ramah, and is situated on a hill a few blocks north of Main Street above the Bond Trading Post.

William Bond, Atheling's father, was John Miller's friend, and often traded horses with Miller and had other business dealings with him. Atheling reported that Miller often patronized the Bond Trading Post in Ramah when he rode into town for supplies, and sometimes would stay overnight in the Bond home, sleeping on the floor by the fireplace.

"Miller used to come into town quite often with other Mexican families," Atheling Bond said. "He always had his hat pulled down and would never let anyone take a picture of him. He was a slight man, about 145 lbs."

Atheling Bond knew that John Miller was Billy the Kid because Miller's wife, Isadora, and Miller's son, Max, had told him so. Also, Miller's old friend, Herman Tecklenburg, who knew John Miller in Fort Sumner when he was Billy the Kid, had told Atheling that the Kid and John Miller were the same man.

Even if he had not been told by Isadora and Max, and Herman Tecklenburg, Atheling Bond said he would have known that Miller was the Kid. "I would have known because of the way he told stories of the exploits of Billy the Kid as if he were doing it himself."

Like others in the community who knew that John Miller was Billy the Kid, the Bonds never told the authorities about him.

"John Miller liked to tell stories about Billy the Kid's gun fights," Atheling remembered, "but he did not want us to think he, himself, was the Kid. He would end each story about the Kid's adventures by reminding us that he was not Billy the Kid. However, his wife, Isadora, who could not speak English, would tell us in Spanish that he really was Billy the Kid, and his name was not John Miller. She told us how Billy was shot in Fort Sumner, and how she took care of his wounds, and when the officers came around to her house looking for him, she hid him between two straw mattresses which she slid under the bed."

Atheling Bond recalls a particular night when, as a young boy, he and a friend, Rulon Ashcroft, spent the night at the Miller home. They had been riding around in the mountains all day, many miles from their homes. The young men knew they could not make it home before night, so they decided to ask John Miller, who lived nearby, if they could stay with him.

When the boys rode up to the Miller house, they were met at the door by a suspicious John Miller pointing a rifle in their direction. "Don't come any closer," he warned. "Let me see who you are."

"We told him who we were fast." Bond chuckled. "Then he invited us in and asked us to stay for supper and spend the night. After supper he started telling us stories about Billy the Kid, and after a while he took off his shirt and showed us where there were twelve bullet holes in his body. Where the shots came out there was a white spot about the size of a silver dollar. Where they went in they were about the size of a little finger."

Obviously, the bullet holes in the body of John Miller made a deep impression on young Atheling Bond. His memory was vivid about the bullet scars. Bond also remembered a long-barreled, notched six shooter which hung on the wall of the Miller home. Young Bond asked Miller about the notches, and Miller replied that he had killed a man for every notch.

Like Billy the Kid, John Miller enjoyed doing tricks with his extra-long six shooter. Atheling Bond recalled that the morning after he and Rulon Ashcroft spent the night at the Miller home, they were standing on the porch when Miller spotted a hawk circling overhead. "See that hawk?" Miller said, and without even taking aim, he shot that hawk right down.

"Then," Bond continued, "Miller said if Rulon or I would throw a hat in the air, he would shoot five holes in it before it landed, and if he failed, he would buy a new Stetson for us.

"Rulon said his hat wasn't much good anyway, and he would like a new Stetson, so he threw his up, and Miller shot five holes in it before it landed."

Atheling Bond also told the story of a time when Miller took a hobbling rope off a shelf at the store and asked a friend to tie it about his wrists, "like you are hobbling a horse."

"Tie it as tight as you can," Miller directed. Then with a twist of his wrist, Miller slipped his hands from the rope. "Billy the Kid could do that," he said with a laugh.

This was the method Billy the Kid used to free himself from various jails, and save his life. It was the way Billy freed himself from handcuffs, and shot his way out of the Lincoln County Courthouse only fifteen days before he was to be hanged in Lincoln.

Atheling Bond, like other oldtimers in Ramah said that John Miller's closest friend was a rancher by the name of Herman Tecklenburg who lived up near McGaffey. "When Miller rode into Ramah for supplies," Bond said, "he would ride on up to Tecklenburg's place, and would spend a day or two with his friend."

Atheling recalled that Miller was at the Tecklenburg ranch one time when he and his Dad stayed there also, and he remembers that Miller and Tecklenburg sat on an old log outside and talked most of the night.

"Tecklenburg told us John Miller was Billy the Kid," Bond said. "Tecklenburg said he knew it was true that Miller was the Kid, and was living right here amongst us."

Tecklenburg also told Atheling that John Miller said he was trying to stay out of trouble, and if no one crossed him, there wouldn't be any trouble from him.

There were times, however, when temptation threatened to overcome all of Miller's best intentions to put his gunfighting days behind him.

Billy the Kid was known as the "fastest gun in the West" when he was operating around Fort Sumner, and John Miller soon established himself as the "fastest draw in the Zuni Mountains." Bond recalls:

"Giles Master, who owned the Master Bros. Trading Post, the only Trading Post in Ramah at that time, had written to his relatives in England about the Ramah area and one of them, a retired British officer by the name of Gore came over. Gore thought he was a pretty good shot himself, and liked to brag about the things he did. He had about sixty head of burros he was driving to Gallup and was going to raise some jennets (a small breed Spanish horse). John Miller and Tom O'Fallon offered to help him drive the burros. On the way Gore and Miller got into a dispute about something, and Gore said: 'I'll just kill you.' Before he could get the words out of his mouth, Miller had a pistol in his face, and Gore begged that Miller wouldn't shoot him."

"I got this story from Tom Hoover who was with the group at the time," Bond explained, "Hoover said that he never saw anyone draw a gun as fast as John Miller could.

"The next day," Atheling Bond continued, "I saw John Miller going by on the hill near the village. So I happened to catch up with him, and I asked him why he didn't go on with Gore and help him take those horses over there."

Miller said: "He got smart and thought he was a gunman and was going to kill me. So I showed him how easy I could get my gun out quicker than he could his."

Bond said that Miller claimed Pat Garrett couldn't have shot the Kid in the chest. "He wasn't a good enough shot," Miller said. "He would have had to shoot the Kid in the back."

Bond reported that Max Miller, John and Isadora's son, told Bond that he knew his Dad was Billy the Kid, and Bond says that today all of Max's kids say they know their Grandaddy was Billy the Kid.

When asked if he liked John Miller, Bond replied:

"Yes, I liked him. He'd do anything in the world to help you. He'd ride fifty miles to warn you if he thought anything would happen to you."

Atheling Bond was born in 1888. Bond said he and his wife, Ina, had a hard time establishing a trading business in Ramah, which he opened in 1911. The Master Bros. Trading Post was already established, and it was difficult for Bond to get credit at the wholesale houses. Eventually, however, Giles Master became tired of the trading business and made it possible for Bond to buy him out. Atheling Bond died in 1980.

The Clawsons

Wayne Clawson and his wife, Minnie Kirk Clawson, were early Mormon settlers in the Ramah-Zuni area. Wayne Clawson owned a ranch in the corridor of private lands between the Navajo and Zuni Reservations near the Miller homestead, and had many business dealings with John Miller.

Blanche Lewis

Wayne Clawson's daughter, Blanche Lewis, age ninety-one, lives in Ramah and was interviewed on October 13, 1989.

Blanche remembered a night she spent in the Miller home when Blanche and her uncle, Louis Kirk, and her brother, Lawrence, drove some cattle to the Miller ranch for summer range. It was late when they got there and Miller asked them to spend the night and share a supper of biscuits and gravy with him. Blanche, who was eleven years of age at the time, remembered that she was frightened because after supper John Miller and her uncle and brother talked "a long time about guns, gunfights, and wild things."

"Lots of guns were hanging on the wall," she said, "and Miller took them down and they talked about shooting them."

Blanche was also distressed with the drinking water from John Miller's well. "The well was lined with cedar logs," she said, "and it was the worst tasting water I had ever tasted."

Blanche said Miller was alone in the house the night she stayed there. His wife, Isadora, and son, Max, were away on a trip. "But the house was cleaned nice," Blanche said.

Blanche was asked if she knew John Miller was Billy the Kid. Her answer was surprising: "Yes, Miller told everyone he was Billy the Kid," she said.

Apparently, Blanche and her family just took it for granted that everyone knew that John Miller was Billy the Kid. Blanche's answer was a surprise because most people said that Miller usually did not admit he was the Kid.

Blanche said her Dad, Wayne Clawson, owned a ranch near the Miller Place, but the family lived in the village of Ramah.

"Miller would often stay in our home in Ramah when he came into town on business or to purchase supplies," she said.

Blanche smiles when she remembers the Miller's son, Max:

"Max was a very good dancer," she said, "and I liked to dance with him when he came into town for the community dances."

Wayne Clawson's grandson, Keith Clawson, who lives in Ramah with his wife Sheryl and three of their five children, was interviewed in October, 1989, about his grandfather and other pioneer ranchers who took up homesteads in the corridor between the Navajo and Zuni reservations in the Zuni Mountains. "They mostly had small farms," he said, "and making a living was hard. You had to grow in the summer whatever you ate in the winter. Welfare checks and food stamps weren't much good in those days."

Keith Clawson's maternal grandfather, Fred Lewis, was the only professional photographer in the Ramah-Zuni area during the early years. Unfortunately for everyone who is interested in the history, scenery, and people of the Old West, Lewis had to give up the photography business because not many settlers could afford pictures in those days, and the process of photographing from negatives on glass plates was time consuming and difficult. Many of his pictures were destroyed through the years, but some invaluable photographs were saved by his grandson, Keith, and some of them are interspersed throughout this book.

Blanche Lewis: Blanche stayed overnight at the Miller homestead when she was a young girl. Her father was a friend of John Miller. Blanche Lewis still lives in Ramah. Photo courtesy of Keith Clawson, 1990.

Emma O. Tietjen
She Bopped Billy with a Bowl of Butter.
The following story appeared in the *Frontier Times* in January 1981. It was written and submitted by Emma O.'s grandson, Warren Tietjen Child:

"When I was a small boy, I used to like to hear stories about my Grandfather Earnest Albert Tietjen and pioneer days, so it wasn't so strange that I should be at the home of his old mining partner Tom McNeil at Bluewater, New Mexico. Tom was 104 years old when he told me this story in the 1950's:

"Earnest Tietjen had been sent by Brigham Young to Sevoya, New Mexico, near present Ramah. He and another man left there to avoid being killed by Indians but returned to settle Ramah when the Indians had tamed down somewhat. He was pursued by Geronimo, who nicknamed him Long Tietjen because he couldn't catch him. The friendly Navajos and Zunis told him when Geronimo or the Apaches would come along, and Geronimo would find a smoking cabin but no Long Tietjen.

"One of Earnest's wives, called Emma O., was alone one day while her husband was out preaching to the Indians. She noticed some men approaching her house. They came in and made themselves at home. Through their conversation she realized she was alone in the presence of outlaws or killers, and felt in a desperate situation. Knowing it would do little good to run, she prepared food as ordered. One of the men seemed to be in charge of the others.

"Making an excuse, Emma went outside and into her cellar and picked up a bowl of butter. Her Norwegian temper flared and she hit the leader over the head with the butter, breaking the bowl with quite a wallop.

"One of the men told her she had just hit Billy the Kid and then asked Billy if he was going to take that kind of treatment from her.

"Billy said, 'I guess I will; she's a woman.'

This incident occurred at least two years after Billy the Kid was supposedly shot by Garrett at Fort Sumner in 1881.

Apparently, John Miller was up to his old tricks, riding around with outlaws and frightening people with stories of gunfights and gunslingers. This story also illustrates the old-fashioned, "tip your hat to the ladies" respect for women that was a characteristic of Billy the Kid and also of John Miller.

*Emma O. Tietjen,
wife of pioneer Earnest Tietjen*

Teen-agers Atheling Bond and Rulon Ashcroft were photographed by pioneer photographer Fred Lewis, showing off the pistol tricks they learned from John Miller. Amused by-stander is unidentified. The camera shy gentleman may have been John Miller dressed in his Sunday go to meeting best. Photo courtesy of Keith Clawson, 1990.

64

Photo courtesy of
Keith Clawson.

*Keith Clawson and his wife, Sheryl. Keith is the grandson of
pioneer Wayne Clawson and photographer, Fred Lewis. Sheryl is
the granddaughter of the early Mormon Pioneer, Ernest Tietjen.*

Fred Lewis and wife Roxi. Pioneer photographer. Photo courtesy of Keith Clawson

Atheling Bond. This photograph was taken a few years after Atheling Bond and his friend Rulon Ashcroft spent a night at the Miller home. Atheling was John Miller's friend for many years thereafter. Photo courtesy of Keith Clawson

Atheling Bond, Jesse Johnson and Rulon Ashcroft, photographed by Fred Lewis showing off pistol tricks taught them by John Miller. Photo Courtesy of Keith Clawson.

Atheling Bond: When Atheling Bond was a young boy, he and his friend Rulon Ashcroft were guests of John Miller at the Miller Ranch house. Later, Miller often stayed at the Bond Trading Post as a guest of Atheling Bond, when Miller rode into town for supplies. Photo courtesy of Keith Clawson, 1990.

Will Bond:
Will Bond was one of the early Mormon pioneers in Ramah. Bond and his sons, Atheling and Joe Bond were all friends of John Miller. Descendants of Will Bond are prominent citizens in Ramah and vicinity. Photo courtesy of Keith Clawson, 1990.

Wilfred and Bertha Ashcroft. The Ashcrofts owned a store near the Miller homestead where Miller often bought supplies. Photo courtesy of Bertha Ashcroft.

Bertha and Wilfred Ashcroft in their home in Los Lunas.

—7—

Max Miller and Friend Feliz Bustamante

S *Children at the Miller Place*
   ome fifteen years after John and Isadora Miller arrived near
Pescado to set up their homestead and start life anew, they adopted a Navajo
boy who was about two years of age, whom they named Max. There are
conflicting stories about the circumstances which surrounded the adoption
of Max.

Feliz Bustamante,[4] a neighbor of the Millers, who lived at the Miller
home for a year when she was a child and is perhaps the only person alive
who is known to have had a close personal relationship with the Miller
family, reports that Isadora Miller told her that John Miller was riding in the
forest one day when he found Max toddling about alone. Miller picked the
baby up, put him in his saddle bag, and took him home.

Isadora told Feliz that his Navajo mother didn't want him, and "she just
threw him away."

Members of the Crockett family, who moved into the area some years
later and established a large ranching operation next door to the Miller
Place, tell a different story. They report that Max was given to the Millers by
his Navajo mother, a member of the Skeet family, because she could not
support him and because the Millers were childless and Isadora was lonely.

Whatever the circumstances, Max was happily welcomed by John and
Isadora Miller. Thereafter, Isadora devoted her life to the little Indian boy,
and he in turn, developed a deep devotion for his mother. Like his Dad, John

---

4. Feliz Bustamante is now ninety years of age and lives in Gallup, New Mexico. Feliz's first
baby boy was born with Isadora acting as mid-wife, and was named Martin. Feliz and her
husband, Climaco Dias were the parents of three other children: Margaret, Thomasito, and
Arturo. Feliz outlived her husband and thereafter was married three times. After the death of
her third husband, Joseph Bustamante, Feliz took a little Navajo boy, whose mother was ill

Miller, Max became an expert horseman and cowpuncher, who learned at an early age how to handle a herd of cattle on the range and to survive the exigencies of life in the wilderness.

During the year 1896, the same year the Millers adopted Max, a Mexican rancher by the name of Jose Manuel Garcia and his wife, Ramona, came to live at Los Pinitos, several miles south of the Miller Ranch. Jose Garcia was a partner of Don Silvester Mirabel, a wealthy businessman and landholder who lived in San Rafael, where Jose Garcia had lived before establishing his ranch at Los Pinitos. These two men were to have a long relationship with the Millers in various business dealings. Also, Jose Garcia, a strict man in all respects, saw to it that Max Miller was properly baptized by Jose and his wife, Ramona. The name that appeared on the baptismal record was Roman Miller. Never mind that, John and Isadora Miller went right on calling their son "Max," and so he was known throughout his life.

Shortly after the Garcias set up their ranch, they brought a little girl, Feliz, into their home to raise as their own. Feliz was the niece of Jose Garcia. Her mother was ill and could not care for her, so the Garcias adopted her and named her Feliz Garcia. When Jose Garcia's wife, Ramona, became ill and died, Garcia sent Feliz who was five years of age, to the Miller home to be cared for until Jose Garcia could make arrangements to bring her home again. John and Isadora Miller took care of Feliz for over a year. When Jose Garcia married his first wife's sister, Aurora, Feliz returned home.

Feliz Garcia and Max Miller were friends even though Max was older. The little girl played childhood games with him while she lived at the Miller home. Feliz, now at age ninety, speaks Spanish. Like Isadora, she never learned to speak English, and no doubt Feliz was great company for Isadora during the year the Millers cared for her.

Feliz remembered that she and Max had many chores for which they were responsible. Feliz recalled that sometimes when the water in the well ran low, Max was required to carry water by horseback from the Atarque water hole, several miles away. Sometimes Max's girl friend, Maria Baca, helped him, and sometimes Feliz went along with them. Max also saw that the wood box in the long room was always filled with firewood. There were

---

with tuberculosis into her home as a foster parent under the Indian foster care program. Feliz loved the little boy from the beginning, adopted him as her son, and named him Herman Bustamante. Herman now attends the University of New Mexico, majoring in languages with ambitions to become a language teacher and writer.

many chores to do at the homestead and everyone kept busy. Animals had to be fed and watered, chickens had to be fed and eggs gathered, crops had to be planted, weeded, irrigated, and protected from predators. Feliz remembered particularly that she and Isadora spent many hours looking for rocks in the forest, which they carried to the fields, where they plugged ground hog and prairie dog holes to keep the varmints from destroying the crops of beans and corn. Feliz remembered, too, three terrible days at the Miller Place when she was kept in a shed because she had picked up a skunk which came into the courtyard to drink at the water tank.

The life of a pioneer was full of hard work, drudgery, and travail, and the children were not spared. If John Miller carried a heavy load trying to protect his cattle from rustlers and the elements, his family carried an equally heavy burden surviving at home. The crops that were so laboriously planted were subject to various kinds of predators, and without the crops there would be no food for the winter and no feed for the animals.

Beside ground-hogs, gophers, and prairie dogs, which ate the roots of the plants, there were attacks by locusts which devastated the plants above ground, stripping the leaves and causing the plants to wither and die. There was drought during the summer months when the irrigation ditches ran low, and there was barely enough water to keep the plants alive, causing a meagre crop.

It was a time when the concept of personal responsibility was a primary guideline for everyone. If you did not work, you would not eat. Everyone understood, and early in life the children learned to put their shoulders to the wheel. There were no excuses and no sympathy for those who shirked.

The Millers fortunately escaped the worst nightmare of all—fire. With little or no protection, many frontier farmhouses, barns, chicken houses and equipment burned to ashes, forcing families to leave and seek a livelihood in a more hospitable place. Then there were the forest fires, caused by lightning or a careless hunter or cowboy who built a campfire and left it before it had burned itself out, or who threw a lighted cigarette into the brush. Over and over again cowpunchers jeopardized their lives driving their cattle to safety from raging forest fires.

Yet, in spite of hardships, Feliz says that she was happy living with the Millers. In a recent interview she reported that the Millers treated her kindly. "They were cheerful people," she said, "and John Miller was always telling jokes and he liked to tease."

" Sometimes," Feliz said, "John Miller would call his wife 'Assadora,' and she would just laugh, because she knew he was teasing."

Feliz said the Millers talked about Billy the Kid a lot but she didn't know who Billy the Kid was, and she was puzzled.

Feliz remembers a tall thin man whose name was Lou Shoemaker, who came to visit John Miller many times when she was staying at the Miller home. "They talked about Billy the Kid far into the night," she said.

Feliz said that sometimes a shorter man came with Shoemaker, and they all talked about Billy the Kid, but Feliz could not understand what they were saying because she could only understand a few words of English. She thought the short man was Billy the Kid because they were always talking about the Kid when he was there. She also thought that the rancher, Lou Shoemaker, was a shoemaker because that was what they called him.

Feliz refers to Isadora as "Aunt Isadora," and says that her Aunt Isadora was good to everybody. Feliz recalls with gratitude Isadora's kindness and compassion towards her the night her first child was born. Feliz said: "I was very sick, and Papa rode over to the Miller Place and asked Isadora to come help."

John Miller drove his wife to the Garcia home and stood by while Isadora delivered the baby.

Feliz's Papa had arranged the marriage between Feliz and Climaco Dias, who was the nephew of Jose Garcia's wife, Aurora. Feliz was fourteen at the time, and Climaco was fifteen. Such arranged marriages were common at the time, and Feliz said: "I didn't have anything to say about it."

In the absence of a doctor or nurse, Isadora served as midwife when Feliz's baby was born, and comforted the fourteen year old mother through her ordeal.

The question is often asked: "Was Billy the Kid a good man or was he bad?"

The answer to that question has to be ambiguous. Billy the Kid was caught up in a situation, not of his making, where he had to decide for himself what was right and what was wrong. When his friend and benefactor John Tunstall was brutally murdered by members of the notorious Santa Fe Ring, who were supported by the government in Santa Fe, Billy chose to take the law into his own hands and avenge the death of his friend the only way he knew. . . by the pistol he wore on his hip. Thus he became an outlaw, and, in some peoples' minds, a murderer. But Billy's friends in the Fort

Sumner and Lincoln areas all said he was a loyal friend and "would do anything to help a friend in need." Similarly, John Miller's friends in the Ramah-Zuni area knew Miller was an outlaw with a dangerously quick temper, who was as restless and unpredictable as a caged mountain lion, but they invariably described him as a good and loyal friend who would ride through the night to help a friend in distress.

Certainly, John and Isadora Miller proved themselves to be Good Samaritans of the Frontier.

Throughout his life, Miller played the hand he was dealt, asking no quarter and giving none, even when the outcome was sometimes tragic. He led a successful life on the frontier under the handicap of being a hunted man who was forced to remain hidden from view. It was enough to ask of any man. John Miller was a credit to the brave frontiersmen who tamed the West.

This dramatic view of Zuni emphasizes the height of both the pueblo and nearby Thunder Mountain, or Towayalane. The mountain is three miles southeast of the pueblo and 1,000 feet higher. (Thayer, 1888.) UNM Press.

Feliz Garcia Dias, son Arturo and husband Climaco Dias. Feliz is one of the few living persons who had a close relationship with the John Miller family. Feliz lived with the Millers for a year during her childhood.
Photo courtesy of Herman Bustamante, 1990.

Jose Manuel Garcia. Garcia was the father of Feliz Garcia Bustamante who lived at the Miller Ranch for a year during her childhood. Garcia lived in Los Pinitos where he owned a ranch and was a partner of the cattle baron, Don Silvestre Mirabel. Photo courtesy of Herman Bustamante, 1990.

Feliz Bustamante and her son, Herman. Feliz lived at the Miller house for a year when she was a child and is the only living person known to have had a close relationship with the Miller family.

—8—

Andrew and Effa Vander Wagen

T he arrival in New Mexico from Grand Rapids, Michigan, of Missionary of the Christian Reformed Church, Andrew Vander Wagen, and his bride, Effa, who was a graduate of the Illinois Training School for Nurses, was an important addition to the Zuni community and to the lives of John and Isadora Miller. The Vander Wagens arrived in Zuni with their baby son, Edward Andrew Vander Wagen on the eleventh day of October, 1897. The only white man living there at the time, was the Indian trader, Charles Graham, who rented a three-room apartment to them. It was the first day of a valiant lifetime the couple spent labouring to convert the Indians to Christianity and helping them build a better life. The Vander Wagens were truly heroic pioneers of the West.

The preacher Andrew Vander Wagen first met up with John Miller under less than happy circumstances.

During the years when Miller's son, Max, was a child, Miller was often seen in the company of other cattlemen, cowpunchers, and outlaws in the village of Zuni. They met to trade yarns and plan roundups at Douglas Graham's store when they came to town for supplies. It was there that Miller bragged he would steal a fine horse he admired, known as John the Flyer, which belonged to the preacher, Andrew Vander Wagen.

John the Flyer was much treasured by the missionary, who credited the horse with saving his life several times when he was in mortal danger. Vander Wagen's granddaughter, Elaine Thomas, wrote about her grandfather and his horse, John the Flyer, and their first meeting with John Miller:

"Scouting the area around Fort Defiance for a mission site, Andrew found the Catholics deeply entrenched in missions at St. Michaels and Ganado. Attempts to establish Protestant missions in such places had been met with extreme harassment from the Catholics. On one such trip to St.

Michaels, however, his time was not entirely wasted. Having an eye for spotting a good horse, he bought himself two wild horses from the missionary there. Mr. Day, a rancher, presented him with an Indian-made bridle and bit as a gift. His purchases were of fiery temper, apparently due to eating locoweed, and on the return trip home, one horse broke away from the buckboard, never to be seen again. The second horse was tamed by Andrew and named John, later becoming known as the "wonderhorse" and "John the Flyer" because of his incredible speed. Traveling ten miles an hour in a trot, Andrew and John the Flyer became close companions in his search of the mission field.

"On Andrew's second trip to Zuni that spring, he was carefully watched by two men as he crossed the Zuni River. Jesus Eriacho and John Miller were admiring his steed and anticipating acquiring it. Outlaws, according to some tales, and only rugged frontiersmen, according to others, their reputations were known throughout the area.

"Back at the village of Zuni, Miller and Eriacho questioned the trader, Douglas Graham, about young Vander Wagen and his horse. Upon finding that Andrew would be moving to Zuni in the fall, John Miller delayed his plans to steal the horse."

If Miller actually intended to steal John the Flyer, it is doubtful that he would have told everyone within hearing distance, but his threat got back to the minister, via Douglas Graham, and Vander Wagen was convinced that Miller actually did intend to steal his horse. When he discovered Miller leaning on the corral fence admiring John the Flyer, Vander Wagen went out to confront him. When Vander Wagen told Miller he had heard that Miller intended to steal his horse, Miller replied:

"Well, to tell the truth, I did intend to steal that horse, and then I discovered that you were a preacher and I thought that wouldn't be the right thing to do to a man of God."

The two men, the preacher and the outlaw, shook hands and were friends thereafter. The missionary, Andrew Vander Wagen, said in an interview he believed that John Miller was Billy the Kid, and he also remarked that he thought Miller was "not right in the head."

It was difficult in those days in the Ramah-Zuni mountains to determine who was, and who was not an outlaw. One native of the area said that "everyone was an outlaw." While this remark may have been an exaggeration, nevertheless it is true that many people came to Ramah and Zuni because of the good water, rich pasture land, range lands and isolation. Many had been in trouble with the law at their previous residences, and were escaping to an area where no law existed. The Navajo Indians still remembered with bitterness when they were forced to surrender to Kit Carson and were marched the long distance to Fort Sumner where they were incarcerated and housed in shacks not fit for animals. Many died before they were allowed to return to the Reservation. The Indians were not likely to turn anyone into the authorities in Santa Fe. The Mormon settlers, too, had been hounded and persecuted by the U.S. Government and would likely be sympathetic to others who had fallen afoul of the law. The general philosophy in Ramah and Zuni was to live and let live, and ask no questions. This is probably the reason that no one outside of the area heard that John Miller was Billy the Kid, although many of Miller's neighbors were aware that he was.

Elaine Thomas reported the following:

"The special hangout for the men in the area, particularly the cattlemen, Indians, and outlaws, was Douglas Graham's Store in Zuni. John Miller and his friends, including Jesus Eriacho, were gathered at Graham's store one day when they were approached by the minister, Andrew Vander Wagen.

"The preacher who had diligently been trying to induce the Indians to attend his church services was becoming discouraged. A young Indian lad, Maricio, was an admirer of the Vander Wagens because one dark night he had knocked at their door and pleaded with them to come help an Indian woman who was thought to be possessed by witches.

"Andrew and his wife Effa dressed quickly. Effa, who was a nurse, grabbed her medical supplies and they followed the young man to the village, where they found four medicine men attempting to hold the woman down because her body was twisting out of control. Effa administered medicine and the young Indian, the preacher, and the nurse started praying in soft tones. The woman was calmed by the sound of their voices and the medicine Effa had administered, and the crisis was over. Maricio was impressed with the Vander Wagens' powerful medicine and thereafter he visited often with Andrew. Maricio became concerned because so few people attended Vander Wagen's services. At one time Maricio made a suggestion to the minister that he should get the white men to attend his church services.

"Andrew immediately took the boy's suggestion to heart, and went to Graham's store where the white men congregated. Several outlaws and noted ranchers were standing around the counter and stillness settled over the store when the minister marched in. Andrew told the white men gathered there that Maricio had asked why the white men did not attend church services.

"John Miller, one of the group, broke the silence by saying, 'Well, boys, if that's what the Indian said, let's help the young man out.' So, either because they had sympathy for the young Indian lad's plea, or because they respected John Miller's suggestion, or because they wished the young minister and his wife well, Anglos and Mexicans from the surrounding area began attending church services in the Zuni schoolhouse."

John Miller, his wife Isadora, and their little son Max often drove the forty mile round-trip on Sunday mornings to church services in the Zuni schoolhouse, to listen to the warnings of the minister, who pleaded with them to change their ways and serve the Lord. It is not clear how much the preacher's plea was heeded, but certainly it did no harm.

John Miller was soon to treasure the loyal friendships he had established with the people of Ramah and Zuni. Their loyalty would be tested. When John Miller needed their support, they would remember the long nights he rode through the Indian and Anglo settlements, distributing cuts of newly slaughtered beef to starving people. Respected citizens like Eugene Lambson and his brother Frank would remember the night they were invited into the Miller home, where Miller cooked supper for them, fed their horses, and sat up all night telling them stories about Billy the Kid. Atheling Bond would remember a similar experience when he and a friend, Rulon Ashcroft, were lost in the woods and Miller took them into his home for the night. Bond would also remember the night John Miller rode into Ramah to warn his father that a Mexican outlaw was planning to steal his horse. Jose Manuel Garcia would remember the night when John and Isadora came to his home to deliver the baby of his adopted daughter, Feliz.

When rumblings began about Miller being in league with the rustlers who were raiding the herds of the Indians and settlers, Miller had support from his friends.

Andrew and Effa Vander Wagen: Andrew Vander Wagen was a pioneer preacher, rancher, and trader, and his wife, Effa, was a nurse. There is no tribute that can do justice to their courage and determination to improve the lives of the people of the frontier. Photo courtesy of Elaine Thomas, 1990.

Elaine and Roger Thomas own the Trading Post in Halona Plaza in Zuni. Elaine is the granddaughter of the missionary Andrew Vander Wagen and his wife Effa.

Christian Reformed Church in Zuni at the present time.

—9—

The Outlaws

The people around Ramah and Zuni were aware of the fact that John Miller was acquainted with many of the rustlers who drove their stolen herds through the Zuni Mountains.

The rustler connection started with John Miller shortly after he arrived in McKinley County and settled near Pescado. Living alone in caves while he guarded the herd belonging to Jesus Eriacho, and later his own herd as well, Miller spent his time riding through the mountains part of the day and all through the night, protecting the herds from predators and searching for rustlers who had picked up cattle that belonged to the ranchers in the area. If the cattle thieves were men he knew, he would ride up to them and demand that they release the stolen cattle. In such cases he always retrieved the cattle, and sometimes he sat around the campfire talking with the rustlers, some of whom had been accomplices of his during his own cattle rustling days.

John Miller was a night man. People in Ramah and Zuni said he never slept. His son Max said, "Nothing ever stirred or moved in the night but what the Old Man knew about it." Miller was at home with the creatures of the night, who, like himself, used the cloak of darkness to hide their whereabouts. He was accustomed to the whir of bats and the screech of owls and nighthawks searching for food in the forest. He was familiar with the howls of coyotes and wolves and the clatter of bears rummaging in the woods for food. Miller felt comfortable in the dark because he was hidden from the view of prying eyes that might reveal his existence to authorities in Santa Fe, who were looking for him and wished him dead.

Anytime anyone came to the Miller home, night or day, John Miller was standing in the door with a loaded rifle. He traveled mostly at night, and the shopkeepers in Ramah and Zuni became accustomed to serving him when he came into town for supplies during the night. Miller knew that he had to escape capture at all costs, because capture meant death by the hangman's noose. Miller had been convicted and sentenced to hang because of his part in the ambush and shooting of Sheriff Brady, and if he were captured, he would also face trial for the murders of two guards he shot when he escaped from the Lincoln County Courthouse jail.

In spite of his best efforts, Miller was not successful in stopping the cattle rustling in the Zuni Mountains, and cattle continually disappeared. The mountains were full of rustlers and there was precious little anyone could do about it.

Atheling Bond reported about one incident when he thought two white men might have been murdered by the rustlers. This is what he said: "My Uncle Joe Bond and I were riding out near Cerro Alto. We were coming home and passed by Tineja and we passed some horses. One was a sorrel and there were two bays and a black. They were not Mexican or Indian horses. Uncle Joe said: 'Well, there was two white men come through Ramah about a week ago. They had these same horses. When they went through here they were going down to the Rio Grande and were going in together to buy some cattle.'

"When we came by the corral at Tineja, we looked in and Uncle Joe said: 'See, they have put those horses in the corral and run them around and around and around. No doubt from the other stories that have been told, those two men are buried in there.'

Eugene Lambson also reported about the rustlers when he was interviewed in 1976. Eugene Lambson's father, Apollas Boaz Lambson, a businessman and trader, was a good friend of John Miller, and did not fault Miller's relationship with the outlaws who came that way. He knew that Miller did what he could to stop the outlaws from stealing from his neighbors. But neither Apollas Lambson nor his son, Eugene Lambson, had feelings of tolerance for the desperados. "They were mostly renegades from Texas," Eugene Lambson said, "They found they could escape the law in New Mexico where they raided the ranches and drove the stolen herds across the state to sell in Arizona.

"They terrorized the countryside," Lambson continued. "They stole cattle, ran off the horses, and killed people who tried to stop them. Everybody was afraid of them.

"One time," Lambson recalled, "Old Man Gallagher, who was Deputy Sheriff at Ramah, saw a fire down in the canyon near our house. He came over to investigate, and we went down to look. It was a band of desperados who were camped there with their saddle horses, stolen cattle and pack horses. We knew some of them—Enos Pipken, Red Pipken, Frank and Skeet Jones, and others. They were real outlaws.

"Another time, a band of outlaws slaughtered a steer out in the canyon for food. Whenever they got hungry they just killed someone's cattle. A couple of Mormon boys, one was named Frank Greer, and I can't remember the other one's name, thought the outlaws had killed one of their steers and rode up to find out. As they came near, the bandits just shot them, and left them lying there. No one could do anything about it because there wasn't any law to force them to justice, and they just did what they wanted.

"Some of the outlaws were headquartered at the 6A Ranch near Vaughn, New Mexico," Lambson recalled.

Cattle rustlers were not the only outlaws who terrorized the countryside, there were horse thieves as well.

Keith Clawson reported a story his Dad, Alvin Clawson, told him about horse rustling from ranches in the Corridor, where John Miller, Jesus Eriacho, Wayne Clawson, Lou Shoemaker, the Crocketts, and others owned homesteads.

"One time," Clawson said, "a band of horse thieves raided the countryside, and rounded up some six hundred horses and had them corralled near Springerville, just across the Arizona border. That was too much for the cattlemen in the area, and they got together and went after the bandits, captured them, reclaimed the stolen horses, and sent for the Sheriff in Springerville. The sheriff arrested the outlaws, and they were tried and sentenced to some ten years in jail. For once justice was done.

"The whole area was infested with outlaws," Clawson said. "There were lots of outlaws at the Box-S Outfit in Nutria, working as cowpunchers. Ranchers hired them and asked no questions. All they cared about was if you could handle cattle. It got so bad, one of the outlaws killed a Zuni man, and finally they had to close down the whole operation."

Historian Gary Tietjen wrote the following story about outlaws at the Box-S Ranch and about the gunslinger, John Miller, in his book, *Encounter with the Frontier:*

"Joe Bond tells of an incident involving his father, William Bond, which happened near Danoff. Bond, who was working for the Box-S Ranch and Peg-leg Carter, who was one of the outlaws working there, suspected that some of the Box-S cattle were being butchered by Navajos. Riding together one day, they decided to split up and make a circle, then meet in a certain place. Bond returned to the appointed meeting place first, and finding some fresh tracks, he started to follow them up. He came upon some Navajos who came up to him very friendly-like then grabbed him and tore most of his clothes off. He attempted an escape, and the Indians ran him a long ways, then roped him. The Indians had a rope around his neck, and were debating on whether to hang him or burn him when Peg-leg Carter appeared on the scene. Bond would not say later whether Carter killed any of the Indians, but that outlaw's fearful reputation with a rifle leaves little doubt that some of them carried his lead to their graves. It is fairly certain, however, that these were not Ramah Navajos.

"Ramah was surrounded by outlaws in those early days. The Zuni Mountains were full of them. There is one deep box canyon, opening out near Nutria, which is called Outlaw Canyon. The steep cliffs that form the walls make crossing it anywhere a nearly impossible feat on foot—much less on horseback. One group of early-day desperados, however, took considerable pains to build a series of wooden ramps down into the canyon, so that horses could be ridden to the bottom. Vestiges of the ramps can still be seen today. By means of these cleverly concealed ladders, the outlaws could vanish into thin air. Doubtless, many a pursuer came to those precipitous walls and paused in wonder and confusion.

"There have been, in recent years, in New Mexico, a number of persons who claimed to have been Billy the Kid. Perhaps the first and one of the more original of these claims centers about one John Miller, a gunslinger who lived for many years in the Ramah area, yet who did not make the claim for himself. There were those who recognized him, and were persuaded by him not to reveal his identity to the law. The story, pieced together from many sources, went something like this: When Billy was shot by Pat Garrett, his body was turned over to some Mexican women for burial. They found him still breathing and substituted for his body in the coffin that of a Mexican man who had died the night before. One woman, Isadora, carefully nursed him until he could be taken by night to Reserve, New Mexico, where he recovered. His brush with death convinced him to leave Lincoln County forever and to live under an assumed name in one of the least populated areas to be found in the West. Thus he came to Ramah and El Morro country and took the alias of John Miller."

Atheling Bond reported about two notorious cattle rustlers who operated around Ramah and Zuni. One, Carl Manning, who stayed with John Miller now and then, told Miller he was intending to steal a horse that belonged to Atheling's Dad.

Miller asked: "Why are you going to do that? They are poor people and that's all they have."

Manning said that didn't make no difference to him, he liked that horse and was going to steal it. So John Miller rode into Ramah that evening and told Atheling's Dad to put a chain around the stable door and put a lock on it. The next night, after John Miller left, Bond went out to the corral in the night, and found the chain filed nearly through.

The other notorious rustler Atheling Bond told about was a particularly vicious criminal, Henry Coleman, alias Shreet Hudspeth. Coleman operated in the Southern part of Valencia County and in northern Catron County, driving his stolen herds over the "Outlaw Trail" via Silver City through Reserve and Quemado and ending up north of Gallup, where he sold the cattle to the Indians and anybody else who would buy them. Then his hired outlaws would re-steal the cattle and drive them over the border into Arizona where they sold them again. It was a pretty slick operation.

This is what Atheling Bond said about Henry Coleman:

"I heard the story from Salty John Cox, once Coleman's best friend, and in the end the deputy who killed him. Salty John once rescued Coleman from an adobe jail in Mexico. The jail was without a roof and the walls were fourteen feet high, and the place was heavily guarded. John Cox rode up very close in the darkness, threw a rope over the wall, and Coleman climbed out. The guards heard the sounds, however, and began shooting, but did not hit anyone. Coleman then settled twelve miles from Quemado and married a young woman who had a fortune in ranches and cattle. Whether he suspected her of infidelity or whether he wished to lay hands on the ranches is not clear, but he laid plans to have her murdered. Letting it be known that he would be away, he had her murdered in company with her foreman Don Oliver. Coleman was brought to trial for the killings but was acquitted."

Some time later Coleman drove some cattle into the Zuni area. It was reported that Coleman sold the stolen cattle to the preacher, Andrew Vander Wagen, and Vander Wagen then sold the cattle to the Zuni Indians in the area. Soon the cattle began disappearing. The Zunis blamed Vander Wagen, and some others blamed John Miller and his outlaw friends. It was reported that Miller had been seen in the company of Coleman, and it was known that Coleman had visited at the Miller home from time to time. However, Old Timers report that John Miller and Coleman "didn't get along," and it was known that Miller disapproved of Coleman's activities in the area.

The preacher, Andrew Vander Wagen, told a different story. Here is the Vander Wagen story as related by his granddaughter, Elaine Thomas: "In the fall of 1906 the Vander Wagens moved to the Z. I. Ranch. The Z. I. Ranch was slightly north of the main road leading from Gallup to Zuni. The wagon pathway dropped from the mountains at Whitewater and twisted along a narrow arroyo which carried the melted snow from the spring run-off and the summer rains to the Zuni River. From the Ranch the road continued down the canyon past a red sandstone cliff called Inspiration Point, then zig-zagged to the left through Trapper's Canyon. Climbing over hills covered with juniper trees (commonly referred to as cedars) and sagebrush, the road continued toward Zuni, which sat ten miles southwest from the ranch.

"Mr. Newman had run a small store at the Z. I. Ranch for a number of years, and Andrew Vander Wagen continued its operation, expanding somewhat into cattle and sheep ranching as well.

"All did not go smoothly at the ranch, however. Sheep, horse, and cattle rustling was widespread in the area. Several Zunis once caught Henry Coleman (alias Shreet Hudspeth) with eight of their cattle, the original brands still intact. Attempting to shirk responsibility, Coleman convincingly insisted he had purchased the cattle from Andrew Vander Wagen at the Z. I. Ranch. Federal agents then swooped into the Z. I., charging Andrew with the theft. John Hill, an accountant, worked for Andrew at the time, and he had kept impeccable records of all purchases and sales of livestock. After receiving testimony from John Hill, the federal agents cleared Andrew of all charges against him.

"A short time later, Andrew confronted Henry Coleman in Frabraes, the trading store ten miles south of Gallup, and accused Coleman of being the thief. Coleman drew his gun to kill Andrew but was quickly subdued by the trader. John Hill, having witnessed the event, was still shaking as he and Andrew rode back to the Z. I. Ranch. 'Did you know they were famous outlaws?' he asked."

John Hill was referring to Coleman and John Miller who was also in the store at the time, and was witnessing the confrontation between Coleman and the preacher. It is interesting to note here that John Hill had lived and worked at the Miller Ranch and was often left in charge of the ranch when Miller and Isadora went to El Paso. John Hill could not have been too frightened of the outlaw, John Miller.

The Indians who had been losing cattle to the rustlers were becoming restless, and the settlers feared the Indians would blame them. The cattlemen wanted revenge, and were determined to take after the rustlers.

Shortly after the rumors started, a Zuni Indian, a messenger from the preacher, Andrew Vander Wagen, rode up to the Miller Place and delivered a message to John Miller. A posse was being formed to confront a group of cattle rustlers who were holed up in Outlaw Canyon, near Nutria, with their stolen herds. John Miller was expected to be a member of the posse.

The next day John Miller rode to the village of Zuni, where he met the rancher-preacher Andrew Vander Wagen and other cattlemen in the area. Altogether some fifteen or so armed cowboys and one cowboy-preacher rode out to Outlaw Canyon where they gathered at the top of the steep cliff.

Some time before, desperados had carefully built wooden ramps down the sides of the cliff, enabling horses and cattle to be driven to the bottom of the canyon, where they literally disappeared from sight. When the posse reached the canyon, they could hear the outlaws below calling taunts to the members of the posse: "Come get us if you can," they shouted, "but you'll meet the smoke from our guns."

Among the outlaws were some of the worst to be found: the leader, Henry Coleman, and Frank Jones, Enos Pipken, Red Pipken, and others.

The posse members consulted with one another about the best way to handle the situation without losing all their men on the precarious way down the canyon wall. It seemed to some that it would not be worth the danger to life and limb, and some wanted to turn back, and try to catch the rustlers after they came out of the canyon.

Then John Miller spoke up: "I'll go alone," he said.

A cowboy broke the silence that ensued. "Are you sure you want to do that?"

John Miller grinned and said: "I'll take my one chance in a million."

Then Miller turned his horse towards the canyon wall and started down the path, calling to the outlaws below: "I'm coming down alone."

To the surprise of the posse members on the rim of the canyon there were no gunshots as Miller slowly made his way to the canyon floor. Several hours passed, and the posse members were becoming concerned, fearful that Miller may have been murdered. At last they spotted Miller driving the cattle before him up the canyon path.

No one ever knew what transpired between Miller and the desperados, but it was taken for granted that the outlaws knew him, and he knew some of them. One more time Miller had acted as an intermediary between the outlaws and his neighbors.

One would like to suppose that the act of bravado by John Miller would have ended the cattle rustling in the Zuni Mountains. But of course it did not. Wherever there were wilderness areas that were used for grazing cattle, there were rustlers who would slaughter an animal during the night, or there were gangs of cattle thieves who would drive a stolen herd across a state line to be sold. The cattle rustlers continued their attacks on the herds of the Ramah and Zuni ranchers, and the cattlemen regarded the situation as just one more adversity that was a part of the price they paid as pioneers who chose to live at the very edge of civilization.

—10—

John Miller and Frank Burrard Creasy

In many respects John Miller lived his life at Miller Canyon in much the same way he had lived as the cowpuncher who was known as Billy The Kid. He was at home on the range tending his cattle, and he was pursuing a profession he loved—raising, selling and trading his well-bred horses. There is much evidence that John Miller and his tiny wife, Isadora, and their young son, Max, were happy in their home on the hillside. Courageous and hard working, the Millers faced life's hardships with great cheer. John Miller was always lighthearted and loved to tell stories about Billy the Kid, show off tricks with his pistol and tease his wife and friends.

Miller's son, Max, reported that his Dad loved to dance, and would often attend the Indian Pueblo ceremonial dances and would ride long distances to attend dances in private homes and community halls in the Mexican and Anglo communities. John Miller taught his son to dance also, and Max soon became a favorite dancing partner of the young ladies in the Ramah area.

But John Miller was no longer a cowhand for hire. At Miller Canyon he owned his own homestead and had access to the grazing rights in surrounding government range lands. Later, as his herd increased, the Millers became more prosperous, and established their own ranch. They added storage and guest rooms to their house, and built barns and sheds for the animals, and Miller hired cowpunchers to tend the cattle on the range, and help with his horse-breeding and training business.

Frank Burrard "Burt" Creasy

One of John Miller's hired cowpunchers was a strapping young six-foot four-inch tall Englishman by the name of Frank Creasy. It must be said that the gregarious John Miller had a way of attracting unusual and spectacular people as his friends and companions, men who, like himself, broke the bonds that bound them and dared to set out for adventure in a new and untamed world. They were men like Herman Tecklenburg, Jesus Eriacho, Eugene Lambson, Atheling Bond, Earnest Tietjen, Andrew Vander Wagen and women like Effa Vander Wagen and Isadora Miller. Frank Burrard Creasy was one such.

Frank Creasy was born in Ceylon, the son of an English colonel who was stationed there. When he was a child, Creasy left for England, homeland of his parents, where he attended school until he was sixteen, an age when the spirit of adventure runs high. Creasy wrote in his memoirs:

"I left England in 1906 and jumped ship in New York. I was sixteen years old when I first headed west, and was looking for a cousin that I understood could be found at an Indian trading post near Ramah, New Mexico. It was while I was working at the trading post that I first met John Miller when he came in for supplies.

"I worked for John Miller for a year and a half on and off, before I learned that he was in reality Billy the Kid (William Bonney).

"It was while we were coming back from a horse drive and had stopped in town for a few drinks that I first learned of his true identity. He didn't get to town too often and when he did he made the most of it. He made me promise not to tell anyone his true identity until after he had passed away. The West was full of tough cowboys eager to make an easy reputation."

Frank Creasy is one of very few people who could remember some of the stories Miller told about his life as Billy the Kid. Here is Creasy's account of how he remembered it:

"The following is an actual account of Billy the Kid as I know it.

"William H. Bonney was born in 1859 in Coffeyville, Kansas. He was three years old when his father died and in 1861 his mother remarried to a Mr. Antrim and the family then moved to Santa Fe and two years later moved again, this time to Silver City.

"The first time anyone really heard of the name Billy the Kid was in 1871, when he was twelve years old. A deputy sheriff apparently insulted Billy's mother for which Billy promptly shot him and then fled to the hills.

"He made his next appearance in Arizona four years later in 1875, when he killed another man in a gunfight and later had a shootout with three Indians and a white man over a dispute in a horse trading deal. He killed all four.

"He made his next appearance in New Mexico during the famous Cattle War of the West, where he was arrested and thrown into the Lincoln jail, from which he escaped, killing his guard and a deputy sheriff in the process.

"He was declared an outlaw and a reward of $10,000 was put on his head, 'Dead or Alive,' so the wanted posters read.

"He did not show up again until 1880, when at the age of twenty-one, he returned to Lincoln to visit his Mexican sweetheart. He was at that time in the company of an Indian boy who was of about the same age and build.

"Hearing that a cow had been butchered and one of the sides of beef hung next door, the Indian stole over later that night to remove part of the meat for dinner the next day.

"Pat Garrett, who was the marshall of Lincoln at the time, and a well known bounty hunter, heard that Billy was in town and along with two of his deputies laid in waiting near the side of beef.

"When the Indian boy stepped up onto the veranda of the house, he was shot down by Pat Garrett, who had apparently mistaken him for Billy. Billy told me once that he and the Indian were dressed alike to confuse people.

"Pat Garrett was afraid of the reaction of the townspeople and immediately buried the body.

"Billy heard the shooting, and after finding out what had happened he left immediately with the Mexican girl, whom he later married.

"Pat Garrett was later killed in a gunfight with an outlaw by the name of Brazel, at Las Cruces, in 1909, but he did collect the reward for Billy the Kid of $10,000.

"Billy was not heard of again until 1902, when he and six others held up a bank somewhere in Montana and got away with $8,000. The money was soon hidden in two different locations, $4,000 at each spot.

"The posse, however, closed in on them and five were shot and two got away, one of which was Jesus Cacouse, who I later knew personally. Billy was badly wounded in the side and had to be seared with a red hot branding iron to stop the bleeding. I saw the scar of this wound myself. Billy stood trial and bought his pardon for $4,000 and I saw this pardon many times after it was framed and hung on the wall of Billy's ranch house. It was under the name of John Miller.

"Billy then settled down and homesteaded twenty-five miles south of Ramah, New Mexico, where he raised horses. While I worked at his ranch I remember three different occasions when the sale of horses would fall off and money got scarce and shortly John Miller would disappear with his old friend Jesus Cacouse and return in two or three weeks with saddle bags filled with gold coins in five-, ten-, and twenty-dollar denominations.

"I helped him wash the dirt off of these coins and was paid my wages with some of this gold and often had an extra twenty-dollar piece thrown in for good measure.

"Billy often told me bits and pieces of his past life while we were out on the trail delivering horses to the various cattle ranches, and when I left to join up in World War I, old John gave me the gun and belt that I now have in my possession."

The relatives Frank Creasy was searching for in Ramah, New Mexico, were Bob and Giles Master, who had also emigrated from England. They had opened the first trading post in Ramah and had established themselves as important members of the Ramah community. When Creasy arrived in Ramah, he was first employed at the trading post owned by his cousins. A short time later he worked on and off for John Miller and established his own home on the Rio Pescado near the Miller homestead.

Records in the McKinley County Clerk's office affirm that Frank Burrard Creasy and his wife, Lily, owned a small acreage on the Rio Pescado near the Miller homestead, which they sold to R. Creasy Master and Giles Master on June 14, 1914, for the sum of one hundred dollars. On July 18, 1915, the records show that Frank Burrard Creasy and his wife also sold some property to Wayne Clawson for the sum of one hundred and fifty dollars.

For almost ten years young Creasy and John Miller, whom he called Old John rode the range together, drove cattle to the frontier towns of Grants and Gallup for sale and shipment, and delivered horses to the ranchers. Creasy and Old John sat around many a campfire where Miller cooked their meals, brewed endless pots of coffee, and told the young man tales of Billy the Kid. It was while they were coming back from a horse drive, after they had stopped in town for a few drinks, that Old John told Creasy that he was indeed Billy the Kid.

Towards the end of his life, Frank Creasy, after he had emigrated to Canada and had become a famous Canadian policeman, was interviewed by John Cosway of the *Toronto Sun*. The following story appeared on May 11, 1979:

"History has it that Sheriff Pat Garrett killed Billy the Kid in 1881 but a retired OPP (Ontario Provincial Police) inspector in Toronto says he worked for the famed outlaw from 1906 to 1916.

"Frank Burrard Creasy, 88, says Billy the Kid was home-steading a ranch near Ramah, New Mexico, using John Miller as an alias when they first met.

'He was a darned good, straight forward rancher as far as I knew,' Creasy told the Sun last night. He said he learned of Miller's true identity beside a campfire one night.

'I don't think he would have told me if he hadn't been liquored up that night,' Creasy said.

"When they parted company in 1916, Billy the Kid gave him a gun and holster, said Creasy, who promised not to reveal The Kid's secret until after his death.

'Well,' he said, 'The Kid died at 73 in 1932 or 1933 from natural causes and a recent article in the OPP house magazine is the first mention of his secret.

'I knew the man well and I laugh at the movies about his life,' said Creasy. 'He did kill a few men in the West but so did a lot of other men. The West was the West. It was no Sunday school.'

During the years Frank Creasy lived in New Mexico, he served as deputy sheriff of McKinley County, and then worked for a while as a scout on the Mexican border. When World War I broke out he left for Canada to join the Royal Canadian Dragoons and served overseas with the regiment.

In 1921, Creasy joined the Ontario Provincial Police, eventually becoming a senior staff inspector in 1949.

In World War II, Creasy again enlisted in the army and reached the rank of major. Throughout his long career, Creasy was credited with many acts of bravery, and became famous as an extraordinary policeman.

OPP Commissioner James Erskine called Creasy "almost the perfect policeman."

If, as Creasy reported, Miller participated in a bank robbery in Montana in 1902, there is no evidence as of now that the people who were Miller's neighbors in the Ramah area knew about it. It is certainly very likely that Creasy's relatives, the Master Brothers, heard about the robbery from Creasy, but if so, they must have kept the knowledge to themselves.

It is true, however, that people around the Ramah-Zuni area were sometimes puzzled, because John Miller seemed to always have money when many of the other ranchers in the area were often without any money at all.

When Creasy learned of the death of his friend Old John, he determined to let the world know that John Miller was Billy the Kid. Creasy knew, as did others to whom Miller had confided his secret, that Miller wanted his story told. Frank Creasy, before his death in 1983, tried to do that. He wrote in his memoirs about his long relationship with Old John and he granted an interview by reporter John Cosway of the *Toronto Sun* and was interviewed by Henry Stansu for an article in the magazine *Review* of the Information Services Branch of the Ontario Provincial Police.

The following article by Henry Stansu appeared in the magazine *Review* of March, 1988:

"At 92 years of age, Senior S/Insp. F.B. Creasy had the distinction of being the oldest retired officer in the history of the OPP.

"His reputation as one of the Force's finest, and a man of integrity, has never been in question. Now his claim to have met Billy the Kid in 1906, twenty-five years after the legendary outlaw of the American West was supposedly gunned down. . . is being examined by historians in the United States.

"According to Creasy's personal accounts made public in 1979, William Bonney or Billy the Kid (alias John Miller) gave the young Creasy his 1880 U.S. Army-issued Colt .45 pistol as a parting gift, several years before Creasy joined the OPP in 1921.

"The authenticity of that classic 'Old West six shooter', now owned by Dan Bartie, of Victoria, British Columbia, has been verified as one of the 200 Colt .45's made by the manufacturer. Bartie inherited the gun from his uncle, who was willed the gun by his friend Frank Creasy.

"To date, American historians maintain Sheriff Pat Garrett killed Billy the Kid in Lincoln County, New Mexico in 1881. But according to Creasy's account Garrett killed the wrong man, concealed the error and collected the reward. . . ."

For reasons unknown, historians in the United States failed to follow up on the leads Frank Creasy furnished about John Miller's claim that he was Billy the Kid.

Frank Burrard "Burt" Creasy at the time he was working as a cowpuncher for John Miller. Courtesy Keith Clawson.

Frank Burrard "Burt" Creasy in his youth was a cowpuncher who worked for John Miller from 1906-1916, and was given a pistol and holster by John Miller when he left for Canada to eventually become a highly respected Senior Staff Inspector for the Ontario Provincial Police.

The famous Colt 45, serial Number 60566, which John Miller gave to his friend, Frank Burrard Creasy, just before Creasy left to volunteer with the Royal Canadian Dragoons as they went forth to serve the cause and defense of freedom in World War I. Courtesy of Gordon H. Muir, Ontario, Canada; Richard Sonny Olmstead, photographer; and special thanks to owner Daniel T. Bartie of Victoria, British Columbia, and Mr. Raymond J. Zyle of Mohawk Arms Inc. Utica, N.Y.

The Englishmen, Giles Master and Bob Master in front of the Master Bros. Trading Post, which was the first trading post in the village of Ramah. Photo courtesy of Keith Clawson.

Mule team and coach in front of Master Bros. Trading Post. Drivers: John and Alex Bloomingfield. Standing: Unidentified woman, Joe Bond and wife Maggie, Colonel Gore and wife. Shortly after arriving in New Mexico from England, Colonel Gore unhappily tangled with John Miller and found himself face to face with Miller's 45 Colt. Photo courtesy of Keith Clawson, 1990.

—11—

Boom Time For Cattlemen

The highlights of Miller's life, as of all other cattlemen and cowpunchers in the area, were the spring and fall roundups. It was a time to get together with old pals, meet new ones, and exchange tall tales of the Indian wars, cattle wars, rustlers, and deeds of daring. Always joking and full of fun, Miller was popular with this group, and no doubt his tall tales could top almost any that were told.

Each spring, Miller, like the others, rode into Zuni on his finest and best-trained horse. He was equipped with a tarp and bedroll and ready to join the other cattlemen and cowpunchers at the big corral.

As a horseman, John Miller, by all accounts, was the best there was. He knew it, and loved to show off his skills at the roundup.

By the time the cattlemen arrived, a cook had been employed and the all-important chuck wagon was stocked with the food cowboys liked—lots of coffee, frijoles seasoned with red chili pods and ham hocks, steaming tortillas, bacon and beef jerky, and of course, fresh beefsteak.

At the designated hour in the early morning, the cowboys with their pack horses and chuck wagon, headed for the range, where for the next few days they rounded up the widely scattered herds and drove them into camp. It was dangerous and strenuous work for the men and for their horses. Often riding at a gallop through ravines and canyons and through the forests of pine trees and brush, they would risk life and limb rounding up just one obstreperous cow determined to go its own way.

By evening the men were tired, grateful for a cowboy meal in front of a crackling pine-scented campfire and a warm bedroll beneath a star-filled sky. "There is nothing in the world to compare," said one Old Timer, whose eyes still shine when he thinks about the wonder of it all.

When the cattle had been rounded up, the cowboys drove them to the camp where the calves were branded with the mother's brand and ear-marked, and the male calves were castrated—the whole operation accomplished in a few seconds. Top cowboys with the best trained horses were chosen to separate the cattle as a caller shouted out the brand of the calves, and a roper moved in to rope the calf and pull it to the brander and marker. When all the calves had been branded, marked and tallied, the herd was turned back on the range and the roundup was over. The cattlemen and their cowboys returned to the ranches, bone-tired from riding for as many as fifteen hours a day. The whole operation was necessary because it was the general rule on the range that any unbranded calf over a year old belonged to the first person who found it.

The fall roundup was held for the purpose of separating the cattle for market. Each cattleman selected the cattle he wanted to sell, and drove them back to the ranch for fattening. When the cattle were ready for market, they were driven to stockpens in the nearby railroad towns of Grants and Gallup. There the cattlemen met with cattle buyers from Chicago stockyards. When the deals were completed, the cattle were loaded into cattle cars and shipped to Chicago stockyards, where they were slaughtered for beef for eastern tables.

The early 1880's was an opportune time for John Miller to establish a ranching business in the Zuni Mountains. There was free land for the taking by anyone who had the courage and stamina to withstand the hardships of the wilderness. There was free grazing for their herds in the government owned mountain ranges. But most important, the Atchison, Topeka and Santa Fe Railroad had been completed by 1885, and the nearby railroad towns of Gallup and Grants offered easy access to shipping.

The long, hazardous, cross-country cattle drives which often ended in disaster, were a thing of the past. It was boom time for cattlemen in the Ramah-Zuni area.

It was also boom time for the rip-roaring railroad towns of Gallup and Grants, where work-weary cowboys gathered with cash in hand to try their luck at the gambling tables, get rousing drunk on the potent whiskey served in frontier saloons, and to compete for the favor of the prostitutes who held out in almost every hotel in town.

Before the completion of the railroad in 1885, the town of Gallup was a stop for the Westward Overland Stage, boasting only a general store (The

Black Diamond) and a saloon (The Blue Goose). After 1881, Gallup became a village, acquiring its name because the paymaster for the railroad was David L. Gallup, and the railroad workers would often say, "We're going to Gallup to get paid."

In the years between the completion of the railroad in 1885, and the onset of Prohibition in 1920, the town of Gallup was known as the toughest town on the Santa Fe Railroad. Indians of the Zuni and Navajo tribes, cowboys from nearby ranches, soldiers from Fort Wingate, railroad hands, miners, ranchers, and traders congregated for wild nights on the town, where there was precious little law and order to say them nay. Adding to the confusion were the dirt streets that turned to mud when the rain fell. Most of the men carried arms for protection, until a law limited that right in 1896.

Elaine Thomas tells of her grandfather, Andrew Vander Wagen's unsettling welcome to New Mexico by the rancher, Dan Dubois:

"Arriving in Gallup on October 10, 1896, the missionary Andrew Vander Wagen and the minister, Rev. Herman Fryling and their wives, tenderfoots from Grand Rapids, Michigan, experienced their first taste of life in the Wild West. Shortly after they stepped off the train at the Gallup depot, as they were unloading their possessions from the railroad boxcar, they found themselves surrounded by one Dan Dubois and a band of horsemen, with their guns drawn."

"Gallup was a boom town in 1896. The arrival of the railroad had given the town its start. The major occupation of rancher and livestock grazer was replaced by mining when the coal fields opened in 1883. The arriving immigrants and Easterners increased the population from 200 in 1880, 1208 in 1890, to 2946 in 1900. The influx of people irritated the local ranchers. Prospectors and eastern land-grabbers interrupted grazing herds; the newcomers sought land, and fights ensued over ownership. As violence became increasingly common, federal agents arrived, attempting to keep the peace. None of the newcomers or the federal agents were welcomed by the old-timers of the area. One of the more defiant ranchers was Dan Dubois, who owned considerable land south of Gallup."

Fortunately, Dan DuBois was not opposed to the arrival of missionaries and ministers into the area. When he learned they were men of God, he ordered his men to holster their guns, and welcomed the newcomers, Andrew and Effa Vander Wagen and the Frylings, and offered his help in their relocation.

Elaine Thomas writes that the Vander Wagens and the Frylings were also shocked when they discovered that the European Hotel, where they were staying, was a brothel, not a fit place for a missionary and a minister and their wives. Then they realized that every other hotel in town was also a house of ill repute. They solved the problem when they found lodging with a Christian family.

In the company of other ranchers in the area, John Miller often drove his cattle into Gallup to sell to eastern cattle buyers. Miller, with cash in hand and lots of places to spend it, did his share of celebrating there. Frank Creasy, who worked as a cowpuncher for Miller, reported that it was after a few drinks in town that Miller revealed to him the fact that he was Billy the Kid. Creasy wrote: "He (Miller) didn't get to town too often and when he did he made the most of it." It is certain that Billy the Kid would have enjoyed the pleasures of the boom town of Gallup.

Billy the Kid was said to have been a teetotaler during his gunslinging years in Lincoln County, but there are several reports that John Miller sometimes imbibed hard liquor, and was particularly fond of a local alcoholic dynamite called White Mule.

Miller's hired cowpuncher, Frank Creasy, reported that Miller was "liquored up" the night Miller told him he was Billy the Kid. And there were other stories about Miller and his liking for White Mule.

Wilfred Ashcroft, one of the few surviving people who knew John Miller, and who is now ninety-two, reported in a recent interview about the White Mule epidemic that hit the Zuni Mountain area and produced havoc amongst the Indian, Mexican and Anglo populations. The concoction was made from a mixture of corn and water, allowed to ferment in large wooden barrels and was then distilled into a clear 180-proof alcoholic beverage in various illegal stills throughout the mountains. It was called White Mule because of its powerful kick and disastrous effects.

Ashcroft and his wife, Bertha, owned a store not far from the Miller Place near Pescado, where John Miller often bought supplies. Ashcroft was appointed U.S. Marshall and he and his partner, Jack Lowe, were given the specific task of wiping out the stills that produced White Mule.

"The stuff set people crazy," Ashcroft said, "but it was prized so much that Indians and some of the settlers would do anything to get it. If they didn't have money, they would trade horses and cows to buy it."

Wilfred Ashcroft told about a day when Miller and Jesus Eriacho were drinking White Mule near his store. One effect of White Mule was to make people who drank it quarrelsome, and it was the cause of many a bloody fight in the Indian community, where people were maimed and even killed. Jesus Eriacho and Miller started quarreling, and Jesus reached for his gun, but Miller got the drop on him before Jesus could get the weapon out of the holster. His eyes steely, Miller put his gun back in the holster. "You'll do that one time too often," he warned. "The next time you draw that pistol you're going to kill me or I'm going to kill you."

Ashcroft said that during the five years he worked as a U.S. Marshall under the Bureau of Indian Affairs, he and his partner managed to put the White Mule stills out of commission. The Indians reported to them where the stills were located, and they went out with axes and chopped the stills up.

Ashcroft, like others in the area, remembers buying and trading horses with John Miller. "Once," he said, "I bought a horse from Miller, took it into Ramah, and traded it for a yearling heifer I needed. That's the way we did business in those days."

Ashcroft also remembered John Miller talking about Billy the Kid at his store. "He seemed to enjoy telling Billy the Kid stories," Ashcroft said.

Bertha Ashcroft said, "Everyone knew that John Miller was Billy the Kid, but we didn't tell anyone because we didn't have definite proof, and besides, we all liked John Miller, and we didn't want to cause him trouble."

Wilfred and Bertha Ashcroft both said that John Miller exacted a promise from his son Max, and from everyone else he told that he was Billy the Kid, that they would not reveal the information until after his death.

John Miller, like Billy the Kid, had a way of obtaining the support of friends and neighbors wherever he lived. As Billy the Kid, he moved freely amongst the inhabitants of Fort Sumner and Lincoln and amongst the little people, Mexicans and Anglos, who lived in adobe huts along the Bonito, Hondo, Penasco, and Rio Grande rivers even after there was an award posted for his arrest. The people fed and hid him, and lied to the authorities about his whereabouts, and no one, however poor he might be, turned him in for the award money.

Bill Crockett, a rancher whose family lived next door to the Miller Place, also told a story of an almost disastrous instance of John Miller imbibing White Mule. Here's what Bill Crockett reported:

"My Uncle Lawrence and Miller were driving some cattle to Grants, New Mexico, for sale. My uncle went by a bootlegger's and bought a half gallon of moonshine. That night he and Miller set a dead fallen pine tree on fire for warmth, and started drinking the White Mule, and went to sleep. My uncle awakened in the night and noticed the fire was close to Miller's feet, so he got up to move Miller's legs, and the moment he touched Miller, he was looking down the barrel of Miller's .44 Colt.

Miller asked: "What the hell's going on?"

Uncle Lawrence answered: "I thought you were going to burn your feet."

Miller warned: "Don't you ever make that mistake again."

As if natural disasters, White Mule, and rustlers were not enough to disrupt the lives of people who lived in the Ramah-Zuni mountains, there was pestilence, as well. The dread disease of smallpox, which had almost wiped out the first Mormon colony, hit the area again in the year 1898. It was a year after the minister Andrew Vander Wagen and his wife Effa, who was a nurse, came to live in Zuni. The young minister and his wife endeared themselves to the inhabitants around Zuni when they went out day and night to tend the sick and dying. They offered medicine and spiritual comfort to people who lived in the multi-storied pueblo rooms, to people living in hogans in the countryside, and to white settlers in their log cabins, who were dying from the fearful disease.

Effa Vander Wagen reported about the smallpox epidemic:

"During the terrible smallpox scourge of 1898-1899 no doctor came until the epidemic had run its course, and then he only stayed about four weeks.

"The medical supplies which we brought with us proved to be of inestimable value among the Zunis. The medicine brought us in contact with them and we gained their confidence and good will and frequently paved the way for the Gospel message.

"We feel grateful for the small supply of medicines granted us at the beginning so we could in this way pave the way for greater things and point them to Christ, the great Physician, who not only heals the bodies, but also heals and saves the sin-sick soul."

Bertha Ashcroft reports that through the years many people also died from diphtheria because the water wells were contaminated, and they didn't know it. "The diphtheria epidemics were almost as bad as the smallpox," she said.

The people in the Mormon community at Ramah depended upon the Mormon midwives who were trained to administer medicine and nurse the sick and dying. Where there were no doctors, nurses, or midwives, kind-hearted people like Isadora Miller assumed the responsibility of administering a variety of folk medicines and Indian cures copied from the medicine men. It is reported that Isadora was exceptionally successful in caring for people who were seriously ill.

"Some of the remedies may now seem bizarre, but apparently they worked. Yarrow leaves made into a tea broke a fever. Open sores which would not heal were treated with poultices, among them fresh cow manure, still steaming with animal heat. Rattlesnake bites were treated by killing a chicken and placing the still-warm flesh on the wound to draw out the poison" *(Encounter in the Frontier,* by Gary Tietjen).

A L C Outfit: These cowboys are typical of the men the cattlemen in the Zuni mountains hired. This picture was taken in 1891. None of the men have been identified. Photo courtesy of Keith Clawson, 1990.

Round-up camp in the Zuni Mountains: This photo, taken in the 1880's is typical of the ranchers and cowboys who held round-ups in the spring and fall of each year. It is not known if John Miller is in this group. Photo courtesy of Keith Clawson, 1990.

—12—

The Native Americans

T he Miller Place, situated between the village of Ramah and the Zuni Pueblo, and bordered by the Navajo and Zuni reservations, was ideal for John Miller to do business with both the settlers in Ramah and the original inhabitants of the region—the Zuni and Navajo Indians. It was a fortunate coincidence for the Millers that one of the first men they met up with on their arrival in the Zuni Mountains was Jesus Eriacho, a man of consequence in the Zuni Community, who had established himself as a prosperous and successful rancher and who eventually became governor of the Zuni Pueblo. Eriacho was first elected governor in 1891 and was elected again in 1907.

John Miller and Jesus Eriacho were flamboyant people, unusual in personality, and at the same time capable and fearless. Although Eriacho was some twenty-four years older than Miller, they hit it off at once and established a lifelong, if somewhat turbulent, relationship.

Although the Mormons had not yet established their permanent settlement at Ramah when the Millers arrived, the Zuni and Navajo Indians had been in their pueblos for hundreds of years. The present pueblo of Zuni is the only survivor of a group of Zuni pueblos in existence at the time of the Spanish conquest of New Mexico. They were called the Seven Cities of Cibola because of the stories the early explorer Cabeza de Vaca and his Moorish companion, Estevan, told of the Cities of Gold they had found amongst the Zuni Indians in Arizona and New Mexico. The wild stories these two men told when they returned to Mexico in 1536 were enough to launch an extraordinary expedition, led by Francisco Vasquez Coronado. At great cost, several hundred Spaniards, over a thousand Indians, equipped with thousands of horses, swine, sheep, rifles, six swivel guns and ammunition, set out for the Zuni wilderness area of New Mexico to locate the Seven Cities of Cibola. It must have been a great shock to find the Zuni Indians living huddled together in multi-storied adobe pueblos and rural huts barely managing a meager existence.

Undaunted, however, the expedition pressed on and finally reached the banks of the Rio Grande near the present city of Albuquerque, where they took over an Indian pueblo and encamped for several years, pondering what to do next. In 1542, six years after Cabeza de Vaca had told his story of riches in New Mexico, Coronado returned to Mexico. But that was not the end of it.

After Coronado, the Spanish Conquistadores came to conquer New Mexico and were accompanied by the Franciscan Fathers, who came to civilize the native Indians and to convert them to Christianity.

Missionary work among the Zunis started in the year 1629, and in spite of frequent tragic setbacks, churches were built in three of the pueblos, Hawikuh, Halona, and Kechipanan.

The Pueblo Uprising in 1680, organized by the Indian, Pope, drove the Spanish settlers and the Franciscan Fathers from the missions and Spanish settlements all across the Territory of New Mexico. The Spaniards who survived were forced to return to Mexico. The churches the Franciscan Fathers had so laboriously built were burned. The Franciscan Fathers were killed.

In 1882, when the Millers arrived in the Zuni area, they found only one pueblo, the Zuni Pueblo, which had been rebuilt over the ruins of the old pueblo. It was a greatly diminished tribe that had been ravished by marauding Apaches, had lost their buffalo herds to make way for cattle, and had survived the devastation of the Indian wars. The Zuni Indians had even survived the occupation of their pueblo by U.S. soldiers who were stationed there to protect the Zunis from raids by the Apache tribes. The soldiers, however, consumed provisions that the Indians could ill afford to spare, and no doubt caused more hardships for the Indians than they prevented. The Zunis lived in adobe or mud and stone huts and multi-storied adobe rooms clustered about a plaza. Outside the village they lived in huts with beehive shaped outside ovens called hornos, where they baked their bread and cooked their meat. Some still lived in the primitive pithouse which was a hole dug in the ground, lined with rocks and topped with logs and soil. The Indians built a fireplace on the floor and fashioned a mud and rock chimney reaching to the ground above.

Gary Tietjen, in his book, *Encounter with the Frontier*, wrote about two Mormon missionaries who found sorely needed shelter in a pithouse near Pescado in the year 1876, some five years before the arrival of John and Isadora Miller:

"Ammon Tenny and R.L. Smith were traveling from Isleta to Zuni. The snow lay deep on the ground and a bitter wind blew into their faces. It was not long before the pair were brought to the verge of death by freezing. Finally, their horses could carry them no further. Night was coming on and the two abandoned themselves to their fate. At that moment, however, they saw a strange sight: smoke rising out of the ground. There was no mound, no dugout, no sign of life, only the smoke. They could but wonder if their eyes were deceiving them. Whatever it might be, there was warmth there and they staggered on. They had reached Ojo Pescado, six miles southwest of present day Ramah, and the smoke arose from a kiva-like hole the Zunis had dug in the ground. The couple were taken in, warmed, and treated kindly by the Indians. They never forgot their debt of gratitude to the Indians, and stayed for some time among the Zunis, preaching to them and making converts."

The Zunis tilled the fields around the pueblo by hand and were very dependent upon rain for good crops of wheat, maize and beans which were the necessary staples. They raised cattle and sheep and other livestock to replace the buffalo herds of the past. The Zuni Indians were self-supporting and relatively prosperous according to the standards of the time. Their relatively higher standard of living was partially due to the ingenuity of the Zuni Indians who devised a unique irrigation system which distributed water evenly across the meadows without washing away the topsoil.

The young cowboy outlaw, John Miller, and the Zuni cattleman, Jesus Eriacho, met in the year 1882 and along with the native Indian tribes and white settlers, set out to build a new civilization on the ruins of an old one. By any standard, John Miller and his business partner, Jesus Eriacho, were unusual men. Independent in mind and spirit, there was no way to fence them in. Both were considered outlaws from time to time because they could not adjust to laws that had been passed by far-away legislators who had their own interests and special privileges in mind, and which Miller and Eriacho considered unjust. As unpredictable as the wilderness they lived in, they wrote their own rules, and dealt their own justice.

Mavericks themselves, Miller and Eriacho nevertheless played a stabilizing role in the communities they lived in, partially because both of them were exceptionally intelligent men who spoke the languages of the people they dealt with, and John Miller could also read and write, an accomplishment few men of the wilderness managed. The Zuni language especially posed a problem because it is unique unto itself, there is no evidence that it is derived from any other language.

Neither John Miller nor Jesus Eriacho was bound by ties of race, nationality, religion or culture. They mixed freely with all, often settling disputes between volatile Navajos and Zunis, Mexican and Anglo settlers, Catholics, Reformed Christians, and Mormons. John Miller, because of his outlaw background, also assumed the responsibility of protecting his neighbors from marauding desperados who terrorized the countryside.

John Miller, throughout his life, was at home with Anglo, Mexican and Indian cattlemen. He spoke their languages, relished their foods, sang their songs, danced to their music and he married a Spanish speaking Mexican girl, to whom he was devoted.

Jesus Eriacho told his grandsons, Louis, Seferino, and Tony Eriacho, that John Miller was Billy the Kid. All of their descendants have known through the years that John Miller was the Kid.

Jesus Eriacho became an important man in the Zuni tribe, acting as governor of the pueblo for many years. Jesus was first married to a Zuni girl, and after her death, married a Navajo woman who lived near Pescado not far from the Miller Ranch. He fathered several children by each wife and today there are numerous descendants of Jesus Eriacho living in the Navajo and Zuni communities. The story of Jesus Eriacho is told by people in the Zuni and Navajo communities, and by the settlers who knew him. Some of the stories differ in various ways. The following accounts are derived from interviews with Keith Clawson whose father, Al Clawson, knew Jesus, and by Katherine Eriacho, who is the widow of Louis Eriacho, grandson of Jesus Eriacho, and from a narrative written by the late Lynora Eriacho, the talented great-great granddaughter of Jesus Eriacho.

Lynora Eriacho wrote the following story about her great-great grandfather, Jesus Eriacho:

"Jesus Eriacho, our Mexican blood ancestor, was born between the years 1820 and 1830 in a little Mexican village in Northern Sonora, Mexico.

"When Jesus was about twelve years old, hard years of dry weather and scanty crops came. The father, not being wealthy, but a man of courage, heard of the wonderful land of California and the opportunities that were waiting there. He sold his land, and in the company of some other families started the long trek across the desert of Southern Arizona to California. As was the custom in those days, they took all their horses, cattle, and sheep with them. They moved slowly, letting the stock graze along the way.

"Jesus and his friend, Manuel, who was the same age and the son of the other family, were riding their ponies and driving the stock along as the wagons lumbered over the rough trail. There were no real roads, only the stock trails from one water hole to another. Water was their main problem, so they laced their way across the desert from one watering place to another.

"They had heard about the lawless bands of Apache Indians inhabiting Arizona down to Chihuahua, Mexico. They roamed and raided, plundered and killed, leaving nothing and giving no mercy.

"The Mexican families moved far to the north and thought it would be possible for a small wagon train to get through to California without being molested. This was a chance they had to take.

"For many days the little company moved slowly out of Northern Mexico. They came to the Salt River Valley and there, with plenty of water, let their cattle rest and feed.

"Then one morning, just as the grey dawn was beginning to glow, the peace and quiet were shattered by the terrifying war cry of the Apaches. They came in yelling and shouting so quickly that the Mexicans had no time to arrange a defense. They were completely off guard.

"There is no doubt but that the Apaches had been watching and waiting for this chance—when the little company would least suspect it, and they could come in and make their kill.

"It was all over in a short time. The wagons were burned with all the goods the Apaches didn't want. They were mostly interested in the live-stock. Cattle, sheep and horses were the prizes they were really after. The men and women were all shot down. Jesus and Manuel were the only ones spared. These two the Apaches saved to be slaves. They needed someone to look after the stock and drive them to their new home.

"After being whipped with a doubled rope, Jesus and Manuel were tied onto the backs of their ponies and ordered to drive the cattle.

"For over a week they drove, pushing the stock as fast as they could. Finally, after what seemed ages, they reached a stream in the White Mountains of Arizona. There were a great number of Apache families camped there.

"The two boys were tied up so they couldn't run away. Food was brought to them. It was here they learned that the war party that had attacked their wagon train was a small renegade band, and that the big chief was not pleased with their escapade. However, the prizes that they brought back—the cattle, sheep and horses—were most welcome, and the boys were worth keeping to take care of the stock.

"During captivity the boys were constantly watched and told where to graze the cattle. Once, when they showed signs of restlessness as if they might be planning to run away, they were held down by the braves while others took hot coals and scarred the bottoms of their feet. They were always hoping they would find a way to escape.

"As the months and years went by, they became friendly with an Apache their own age. Gradually a plan began to form. Slowly Jesus planted the seeds and nourished the friendship of his friend until the time seemed ripe for his plan.

"One evening in the spring, friends warned Jesus and Manuel that the braves were planning to kill them. Apparently, the young war party had burned a wagon train again and killed all the whites. They had found some whiskey, and while older men were trying to keep them from going on more raids, the general cry was, 'Kill the Mexican boys.'

"So they decided that their escape had to be that night. With their friend they selected four horses, not the little inbred mustangs but the best Spanish horses the Apaches had been able to steal. They were all dark colored horses, so they wouldn't show up at night.

"Jesus and Manuel knew they couldn't spare the horses, but must ride as fast as they could. They led them slowly away until the sound of their hoofs could not be heard in the camp. When they were out of hearing, they let the horses have their heads.

"These were sound horses, high spirited and anxious to run as fast as they could over the rough terrain.

"They traveled toward the east and the top of the White Mountains. As the sun came up, they stopped for a moment to decide which way they should go. Manuel wanted to go back to Mexico. Jesus tried to convince him that it was too far without water, and that the Apache bands roaming toward the south were sure to find him.

"Jesus had heard of some friendly Indians up to the north and he wanted to take his chances with them. Both boys knew that the Apaches would be after them as soon as they were missed. But the two boys parted near St. Johns, Arizona, and never saw or heard of each other again.

"All morning Jesus rode without slackening his speed. He crossed a little brook, stopped to let his mounts have just a sip of water. They were too hot to have very much, and there was no time to let them cool off. He knew he must keep moving and as he did so, he kept looking back to see if anyone was following.

"The horse Jesus was riding was slowing, and beginning to stumble. The long slopes were harder and harder for him to climb; but Jesus knew he couldn't spare the horses. His own life was at stake.

"Finally, the horse stumbled for the last time and Jesus mounted the horse he had been leading. He rode all night, covered many miles, but was exhausted. Still, he knew he must get as far away from the Apaches as possible. He was going into the second day. It was beginning to get light in the east. His horse began to stumble. He could not go much farther.

"They came to a stream which is now called Ojo Caliente, south of Zuni Village. Jesus and the horse had to rest before they could go on.

"At that instant, an Indian was standing over him ready to grab him. In his tensed mind he thought, 'Has this awful journey been for nothing?' He was sure the Apaches had caught up with him. Then he noticed that this man was not dressed like an Apache. When he tried to rise, the man pinned his arms to his sides. He was too tired to struggle.

"Jesus couldn't understand what the man was saying. He tried to speak to his captor in Apache, but the man shook his head. When he spoke in his native Spanish, to his surprise, he was answered.

"Jesus learned that he was in the land of the Zuni Pueblo. These were the friendly Indians he had heard about. He explained that he was Mexican and that he had been captured by the Apaches. Since the Apaches were long time enemies of the Zunis, the two had something in common.

"The Zunis accepted him into the village. Since the village chieftain and his wife had no children of their own, they took him to their home and cared for him. This made it easier for him to be accepted. They became his Zuni father and mother. Jesus helped around the house, carrying water and getting wood.

"Work did not mean much to Zuni boys and men. They were hunters and fighters of enemies. When Jesus began doing women's chores, the young Zunis picked on him and called him squaw. He ended up hitting them with his fist, which was a new way of fighting to the Zunis. The young ones complained to the councilmen and the councilmen met with the Chief.

"The meeting lasted into the night. At the conclusion of his special meeting, Jesus explained that he had done Zuni women's work because where he was born in Mexico the men and boys did all outside work while women took care of house chores. The Zuni council finally agreed that this system should be tried, and the Chief took all responsibility for the conduct of Jesus. The councilmen then recognized Jesus as the adopted son of the Chief.

"Time passed. Jesus taught the Zunis how to carry water the way his people in Mexico did, and it was approved by the council. Instead of carrying water a little at a time on the head, he made stout rawhide straps and hung two ollas, one on each end of a strong stick placed across the shoulders. The boys were not good at carrying water on the head, but they could carry it with the yoke.

"With several years of living with the Zunis, he gained much knowledge of the ways of the Pueblo people. He gained the respect of the people and became one of the leading men of the village.

"Then came the time when the old Chief was no more. The councilmen met to pick a new chief. Since ordinarily the chief's son would take over, and since Jesus was married to a Zuni girl, the councilmen wanted Jesus to be their new chief.

"Jesus was made Chief of Zuni Pueblo and started planning and accomplishing things through cooperation with non-Zunis, such as Anglo homesteaders and other Indian tribes. He took trips to Washington, D.C. to regain some of the land. He gained lots of respect and recognition, and kept and respected Zuni traditions and culture.

"As he got older, Jesus started buying land and homesteaded some. He settled at Jack's Lake, which is at the eastern end of the Zuni Reservation, and also obtained farm land west of Ramah in the Pescado area, which his grandson Jefferson Eriacho still occupies. The homestead at Jack's Lake is also occupied by his grandson.

"Jesus also owned part of Ramah Valley, which he sold to the late Lawrence Clawson, the father of Kirk, Alvin, Darrell and Leslie Clawson.

"Jesus raised cattle, sheep and race horses, and his grandsons are still running some of these fine horses.

"In early 1905, after his Zuni wife died, there was a family residing near Jack's Lake and he married a daughter of the family. Of the Navajo marriage, there were four children: Frank Jesus Eriacho, Mrs. Jennie Pino, Mrs. Florence Marine, and another son who froze to death when he ran away from Fort Wingate School in 1933, the year of the deep snow.

"Frank Jesus Eriacho's children in Ramah are: Franklin Eriacho, Chimeco Eriacho, Cecil F. Eriacho, Leonard J. Eriacho, Ethel Lee, Angeline Lee, Esther Martinez, Dorothy Antonio, McDaniel Eriacho, Kenneth L. Eriacho, Allison Pokagon, Herbert Eriacho, Margaret Shorty, and Frank E. Paul.

"Jesus died in the 1930's while hauling lambs to the market. He fell out of a truck and it ran over him. He was around one hundred years old." (Written by Lynora Eriacho for *TSA' ASZI'* Magazine, Fall-Winter, 1984.)

The following account of Jesus Eriacho was reported by Katherine Eriacho:

"Jesus said that the Apaches were cruel to him and his friend, Manuel. The squaws beat them for the slightest offense, and to prevent them from running away, the warriors stabbed them in the calf of the leg with a knife and left the knife in the wound, threatening to slit the boys' throats if they removed it. First they stabbed one leg, and if the wound started to heal, they stabbed the other leg. One time when the warriors thought the boys were becoming restless and might run away, they held the young boys down and burned the bottoms of their feet with hot coals.

"A young Apache girl felt sorry for the boys, and told them to meet her outside the camp one evening and she would help them catch four horses and would bring them some jerky, and they could escape their captors. The girl kept her promise. 'Ride north and do not spare the horses,' she advised. 'At daybreak they will discover you are gone and will be looking for you.'

"The boys did as they were told, and rode through the night towards New Mexico as fast as their horses would run. They rode for two days, and had stopped to water their horses at a pond when the horse Jesus had been riding dropped dead. The horse was too hot and too tired, and the cold water killed him. Jesus continued on north at a trot because his remaining horse could not go any faster. At some point his friend, Manuel, decided to go back to Mexico and turned south, and the two friends never saw one another again.

"Jesus reached the Zuni Reservation in Northern New Mexico, and dismounted to drink at a stream. When he stood up, he was captured by a Zuni man, Charlie Jesus, who had been watching him. Charlie Jesus took the little boy to Ojo Caliente where Charlie was farming. When the Apaches came looking for Jesus, Charlie Jesus hid the boy's horse in the mountains and hid Jesus in the basement of his house. The Apaches looked for the boys for several days, and then returned to Arizona. Charlie Jesus and his wife had no children of their own so they adopted the boy, named him Jesus Eriacho, and raised him to manhood. At that time, many of the Zunis had been converted to Christianity by the Franciscan Fathers, and the name 'Jesus' was popular as a first name and last name as well.

"All through his life, Jesus's leg was scarred and twisted from the knife wounds and burns the Apaches inflicted upon him."

Keith Clawson said his father, Al Clawson, told him that his father, Wayne Clawson, would sometimes help with the cattle at Jesus's ranch when Jesus was an old man and could no longer ride with the other cowpunchers. While his Dad was working, young Al Clawson was in the house with Jesus Eriacho, and the old man entertained the little boy with stories of his capture by the Apaches. Al Clawson never forgot, and told the stories to his own son, Keith.

There are conflicting stories about Jesus's racial heritage. Some say he was part Yaqui Indian, but Keith Clawson and Katherine Eriacho both say they were told he was of Mexican descent. Jesus had light skin and blue eyes, which would indicate that he may have been a descendant of one of the early Spanish explorers who came to Mexico from Spain. (The death certificate of Jesus Eriacho lists his race as "white.") Whatever his racial background, there can be no doubt that Jesus Eriacho's heart belonged to the Zuni and Navajo Indians who cared for him, raised him to manhood and mothered his children.

By the time John and Isadora Miller arrived in the Zuni Mountain area, Jesus was already buying ranches along the corridor of private lands between the Navajo and Zuni Reservations, and was becoming established as a prosperous cattleman and important person in the community.

Eventually Jesus owned four deeded ranches: Broken Windmill, the Padilla Place, Norfleet, and a ranch that he bought from Rosy Castillo. He willed them all to his son Louis Leopollo Eriacho.

Katherine Eriacho tells of the death of Jesus Eriacho:

"After serving as governor of the Zuni Pueblo, Jesus returned to his farm at Ojo Caliente. He was an old man, near ninety years of age, when he was called back to Zuni to settle a dispute. He complained that the night before he had a bad dream which caused him to be fearful. His grandson, Louis, went after him. Jesus was sitting by the outside door of the truck as they were driving back to Zuni. Somehow the door of the truck flew open, and he fell out. His neck was broken by the fall and he was taken to the Public Health Service hospital in Zuni, where he died."

Jesus Eriacho died in the year 1933.

Katherine Eriacho said her own father, Jesus Arviso, a Mexican lad from Sonora, Mexico, also had the misfortune to be captured by Apaches and was brought to the White Mountains, where he was treated as a slave by the Apaches.

Katherine reports about her father's rescue by Navajos from New Mexico:

"New Mexico Navajos traded back and forth with the Apaches and one time the Navajos went over there and traded a black horse for my father, Jesus Arviso."

Katherine says she has a picture of her father, Jesus Arviso, taken at the time of his capture. "He was a dark and sad little boy dressed in a black suit and wearing a black hat," she says. The Navajos brought Jesus Arviso back to the Navajo Indian Reservation, where he was raised to manhood.

Jesus Arviso learned to speak Navajo and English besides his native Spanish, and became an interpreter for the U.S. Army at Fort Defiance. Later, Jesus Arviso owned a ranch at Coyote Canyon and lived at Tohatchi, where he married and raised his family.

Katherine Eriacho is the niece of the famous Navajo Chief Chee Dodge.

Beehive shaped oven, or "horno," is seen at Indian pueblos. (Thayer, 1888.) UNM Press.

Chimeco Eriacho—Great grandson of Jesus Eriacho.

*Lynora Eriacho—Great-grand-
daughter of Jesus Eriacho,
who was Governor of Zuni
Pueblo and friend of John Miller.
Lynora was tragically killed in an auto
accident when she was still researching
the life of her ancestor, Jesus Eriacho.*

*Catherine Eriacho, widow of Louis
Eriacho, who was the grandson of Miller's
long-time friend and business partner,
Jesus Eriacho. Catherine Eriacho lives in
Zuni Pueblo.*

Victorio, one of the greatest Apache war chiefs, was killed in an ambush in Mexico in 1880. (Ladd, 1891.) UNM Press

Geronimo just before his surrender to Gen. Miles, from a photograph taken during an earlier conference with Gen.Crook. (Harper's Weekly, April 10, 1886.) UNM Press

Shalako ceremony is Zuni's best known and most magnificent one. Held each December, it lasts all night. (Century, February, 1883.) UNM Press

View of Zuni shows prominent stake corrals. (Schoolcraft, 1856.) UNM Press

"The Apaches are coming!" A New Mexican Paul Revere spreads the news to isolated "ranchos" in this dramatic early drawing by Frederic Remington. (Harper's Weekly, Jan. 30, 1886.) UNM Press

Navajo shepherdess tends her flock in solitude on the reservation.
(Brooks, 1887.) UNM Press

Atop El Morro rock are the ruins of an earlier pueblo, still visible to the tourist who
climbs the landmark that is now a national monument. (Whipple, 1856.) UNM Press

—13—

Arrival of The Crockett Families

By the year 1914, the free and easy acquisition of land in the west was coming to an end. The days were gone when people could settle on a piece of land, prove up, and call it their own. In keeping with changing times, John Miller filed for a homestead patent on 160 acres at Pescado, which was granted by the Federal Land Office and recorded in the Gallup, New Mexico, County Court Records on May 25, 1914. On the same day, John Miller deeded the homestead to his wife, Isadora.

On November 26, 1915, John and Isadora Miller sold the homestead of 160 acres for the sum of five hundred dollars to Silvestre Mirabel, a wealthy landowner who lived in San Rafael. Silvestre Mirabel was a cattle baron of the West, who ran herds of cattle from Arizona and Colorado to market in New Mexico.

After the sale of his homestead to Silvestre Mirabel, John Miller essentially became a sharecropper on his old homestead, sharing the proceeds of his work with Jose Manuel Garcia, who was a partner of Silvestre Mirabel. There is no indication that there was anything questionable about the transactions between Mirabel, Garcia and Miller. Rather, the sale of the homestead was the result of circumstances over which the Millers had little control. The owners of small herds, who held limited acreages on small homesteads, were finding it harder to earn a living. The price of beef had dropped, there had been a series of drought summers, the lifesaving springs were drying up, and John Miller was getting old. He could no longer ride in the saddle most of the day and night on the range as he had done in his younger days. The herd was cut down to the few cattle he could maintain at the homestead, and he and Isadora devoted their time to raising corn and beans, a few vegetables, chickens, and of course Miller's beloved horses.

Don Silvestre Mirabel, taking advantage of changing economic conditions, devised a unique plan for getting his cattle herds to market in New

Mexico. He bought out small ranchers like John Miller, and then worked out a sharecrop partnership, where the ranchers would agree to furnish water and feed to get the cattle ready for market when they were driven through the area. Mirabel established a network of such small ranchers all along the routes he drove his cattle. Apparently it was a successful plan because Mirabel became a very wealthy man. He lived in a mansion at San Rafael which still stands, and is a reminder of a style of life in the Old West that few people enjoyed.

The Miller's son, Max, was growing up, and like all young men was anxious to be out on his own. He found his opportunity when, in 1916, the Crockett families from southeastern New Mexico bought several large ranches adjacent to the Miller property, and Walter Crockett and his wife and their three daughters built a ranch house within a mile of the Miller Place.

In that year, Max Miller, who by that time was in his teens, went to work at the Crockett ranch as a cowpuncher. Max may have had ideas of getting married when he was settled in a job that paid wages. His childhood friend, Feliz Bustamante, reported that Max was very much in love with his girlfriend, Maria Baca. "They were always together," Feliz said, "and I think they would have married, but Max went off to war. While he was gone the girl he left behind married someone else."

Walter Crockett's daughter, Jewel Crockett Lambson,[5] reported on the arrival of the Crocketts south of the Zuni Mountains:

"In 1916 the Crockett families from southeastern New Mexico sold their ranches and moved to Gallup and points south. Grandmother Crockett moved with seven of her eight children and their families, bringing all their earthly possessions: wagons, Model T Fords, dishes, furniture, children, cattle, horses, mules, and dogs.

"Our ranches were located fifty miles south of Gallup, fifteen miles from the Mormon settlement of Ramah. We bordered the Zuni Reservation, Navajo settlements, several Mexican families who were long-time residents there, and John and Isadora Miller, whose property, known as the Miller Place was adjacent to ours.

"My grandmother, Mary Jane, was so excited over the plentiful supply of wood everywhere. At last she had escaped the Great Plains, with their

5. Jewel Crockett Lambson , who lives in Elephant Butte, N.M., has done much of the research on this book, and owns two pictures of John Miller when he was a rancher at Miller Canyon.

supply of mesquite roots and cow chips. She did not realize how rugged life could be in our new surroundings. At that time my oldest sister, Rena, was six years old, I was three, and Agnes was six months old. My mother was twenty-five, and my Dad was thirty-five. We were all camping at a place called the Norfleet Place. We had just arrived when I fell off the car and broke my arm. My Aunt Minnie and her daughter Velma started walking down the road hoping to find some help. Fortunately, they met a man named Jesus Eriacho."

The ubiquitous Jesus Eriacho, the same man who rescued John and Isadora Miller some thirty-four years before, and who owned the Norfleet Place where the Crocketts were camping, was there to help the little Crockett girl with the broken arm. Jesus made splints and then set the arm. Jewel reports he also said a prayer and then spit on her arm before he bandaged it with long pieces of sheet. Jewel said: "My arm has been perfect all of my life although it was broken at the elbow."

The Walter Crocketts settled on the Shoemaker Place, which no doubt had belonged to John Miller's old friend Lou Shoemaker. Jewel's Dad, Walter Crockett, often stopped by the Miller Place and reported that John Miller was definitely an outlaw because he sat in his front door, gun in hand, day and night. Later, the Crocketts all became convinced that John Miller was Billy the Kid.

Jewel reported about their new friends John and Isadora Miller and their son Max:

"Max Miller soon came to live at our home to help the cowboys and to attend our little 'home' school, where he learned to read and write. My cousin Kate had graduated from high school and Dad hired her to teach us— all girls except Max, which he didn't like much. He would rather have been out working with the cowboys.

"Sometime after Max came to live with us, he finally told us that John Miller was actually Billy the Kid. He said his Dad was 'on the dodge' and had spent several years hiding in caves near our home. His Mexican wife, Isadora, carried food to him regularly. I have seen one of the caves, and have taken pictures of it, as it was so close to our home.

"After a short time, all the Crockett men became acquainted with John Miller and had many business dealings with him. Miller and Isadora took frequent trips to El Paso by wagon, and my folks always were very curious about that because the Millers always traveled at night, and the trails were very dangerous and difficult. John Miller finally confessed to my Uncle Andrew that he was Billy the Kid and that was the reason he always traveled at night."

Andrew Crockett, who was one of the very few people to whom John Miller confided that he was Billy the Kid, was a prominent rancher and later became Sheriff of McKinley County.

The late Rena Crockett, eldest of the three Crockett girls, was interviewed in 1976, and recalled one night when John Miller came to the Crockett home looking for medicine for his wife Isadora, who had caught her hand in a trap she was setting for gophers and had torn her fingers badly.

Miller said: "I have to save her life because she saved mine more than once."

Rena also remarked that she thought John Miller was a "nice looking man, who was a very good dancer."

The Crocketts were all musical, and Walter Crockett joined Eugene Lambson to form a country band that played for dances in the village of Ramah. Bertha Ashcroft said that everyone in town looked forward to the Saturday night dances when the Crocketts came to town to play for community dances at the village hall. Eugene Lambson played a mean fiddle and Walter Crockett played the guitar, and John Miller was often in attendance, delighting the ladies with his dancing ability.

Walter Crockett's youngest son, Bill Crockett, who was born after the Crockett family moved to the Ramah area and has been a lifelong rancher and barkeeper in the Ramah-Zuni mountains, reports that his father told him of an incident concerning John Miller which occurred shortly after the Crocketts arrived in the area:

"According to my father," Bill reported, "John Miller came to our home late at night, and was all shook up. He asked for a good fast team of horses and a buckboard. He said his wife had turned ill and he needed to take her to a doctor. He told my father that his wife had saved his life more than once and he could not let her down. My father gave him our best team, and a buckboard and he took his wife to a doctor in Magdalena, New Mexico, where she recovered from her illness. Miller returned the team and buckboard and seemed indebted to my father after that. Any favor that was asked of Miller was fulfilled immediately. One dry summer there was only one well in the whole area that was producing water, which was watering all the livestock. The well was being pumped day and night, and the pulley belt wore out and was no longer useable. Miller came by a little after sundown and my father commented that he would have to go to Ramah in the morning for a new belt. Miller volunteered to go that night. He was back next morning before daylight with a new belt, a good thirty-mile trip by horseback. My father asked how he managed to get in the store at night, and Miller said: 'They always take care of me at night.' All of the Old Timers in Ramah surely believed that Miller was Billy the Kid and knew that was the reason he traveled at night."

The Crocketts were grateful to John Miller for many favors, but one in particular stands out. Jewel reports:

"When my baby sister was a toddler, all the family was involved in morning chores; so many cattle and horses to be tended, and cows to be milked. My Mom usually milked, but at times my Dad helped. They were surprised one morning when John Miller rode up with their baby. He had found her a mile from home, going up the trail into the forest, and Miller had brought her home."

Max Miller lived with the Crocketts until World War I broke out on April 6, 1917. When the United States declared war against Germany, Max reported to work at Fort Wingate, near Gallup, which had been reactivated for recruitment and training of soldiers. Shortly afterwards, Max was drafted into the army and was sent to Germany.

Jewel's cousin, A.J. Crockett, who now lives in Virginia, reported about Max Miller's first day on the job at Fort Wingate: "When Fort Wingate was reactivated at the beginning of World War I, many local civilians were hired to work there. Among them was Max Miller. The first day Max reported for work he was in the office. Someone had hung a picture of Billy the Kid on the wall, and a fellow employee asked Max: "Do you know who that is?"

Max replied: "Yes, that's my Dad," and went quietly on with his work.

During the time Max lived with the Crocketts, a lifelong friendship was formed with the Crockett family, and particularly the younger Crockett son, Bill Crockett. The Crocketts all report they loved Max like a brother. Jewel said he was always quiet and mannerly and laughed a lot. "When he got sick with diphtheria," Jewel said, "my mother doctored him like he was her own son. We were all raised without a doctor, but pioneer women knew many folk remedies that were amazingly successful."

Bill Crockett in NM National Guard
uniform at beginning of WWII.

Bill Crockett and Max Miller after
World War I.

Bill Crockett as rancher, barkeeper,
band leader, song writer, and vocalist.

Jewel Crockett Lambson: Jewel's family lived a mile from the Miller home and were friends of John and Isadora Miller. This picture was taken when Jewel was a student at Arizona State Teachers College in 1932.

Walter Crockett and wife Claudia: Crockett owned a cattle ranch adjacent to the Miller property, and was a friend of John Miller. Crockett's son Bill Crockett and daughter, Jewel Crockett Lambson have written their stories about John Miller in this book. Photo courtesy Jewel Crockett Lambson, 1990.

—14—

Last Days at the Miller Ranch

T hings were not going well for the Millers when the year 1918 dawned. Isadora was in poor health, was losing her eyesight, and was showing the devastating effects of a life of hard work and lack of proper medical and dental care. With one hand rendered useless from injuries received when it was badly torn in a gopher trap, Isadora could no longer manage even the routine tasks of heating water, washing dishes, and doing the family laundry with the primitive means at hand. John Miller was suffering the effects of a lifetime on horseback; his bones were stiff and it was difficult for him to swing into the saddle. Then the final blow fell. The U.S. Department of the Army notified the Millers that their son, Max, was missing in action in Germany, and was presumed dead. According to reports of Old Timers, the notice was accompanied by a government check in compensation for the loss of their son.

The meadow the Millers farmed was no longer the lush pasture it had once been. Repeated droughts had dried up the grasslands and there was barely enough drinking water to keep the Millers and their livestock alive. Also, Silvestre Mirabel and his partner Jose Manuel Garcia were demanding their share of a crop that was not enough even to sustain the Millers. Quarrels broke out between the partners.

John Miller made plans to move to a warmer climate where he hoped he and Isadora would recover their health, and where there were friends to welcome them. They laid their plans to drive the long, dangerous mountain trails to El Paso one more time. John and Isadora Miller drove into the village of Ramah and stopped at the Bond Trading Post, where they loaded the wagon with provisions for the trip before driving on up to McGaffey to visit Miller's old friend, Herman Tecklenburg, for the last time.

Tecklenburg was having his own problems with the drought years. He had been forced to leave his homestead, and had gone to work sharecropping with the McGaffey Lumber Company at McGaffey. He raised produce for the lumber men and barley, oats and rye to feed the logging horses. He operated this farm until 1923, when the lumber operations ceased.

In 1923, Tecklenburg moved to Gallup, New Mexico, where he was interviewed in 1944 by the *Gallup Independent* and paid this final tribute to his friend John Miller, alias Billy the Kid:

"I used to hear of Billy the Kid through friends up to about 10 years ago, but I don't know if he is alive today or not. He had lots of friends all over the country, but there was a few who wanted him out of the way because they couldn't handle him. That's why they outlawed him and kept hounding him.

"He was a real man and there aren't many like him anymore."

Mr. Tecklenburg paused for a bit and chuckled: "If Billy's alive today, I can just hear what he'd say: 'They can't even leave me alone now when I'm old and worn out.'"

John Miller's farewells to his friends in the Ramah-Zuni area were sad leave-takings because they knew it was forever. The Millers would not be back.

Miller's long-time friend Jesus Eriacho, after the death of his first wife, had married a Navajo woman at Pescado, and had established a ranching career on the Indian Reservation, where he raised cattle, sheep, and racing horses. For many years he was governor of the Zuni Nation. There are today many descendants of the charismatic Jesus Eriacho living in the area.

Eugene Lambson left Ramah and took a job elsewhere, but returned after his retirement to establish a malt shop in Ramah. Sometime later, Eugene told an intriguing story concerning John Miller, which happened at the malt shop:

"One day," Lambson said, "a stranger from Phoenix, Arizona, walked into the malt shop. He was looking for an heir to John Miller's estate. He told me John Miller had died in Buckeye, Arizona, and since no one there knew of any survivors, the court appointed three men to go through his effects. The man said he was one of the persons so appointed, and when they searched through the contents of an old trunk, they found documents, letters, and other items which convinced them that John Miller was Billy the Kid."

Lambson directed the man to John Miller's adopted son, Max Miller, but Lambson never learned what happened to the trunk after that. Later, when Max Miller was interviewed about his life as the son of Billy the Kid, he could not remember anything about what happened to the trunk and had no idea where it was.

The Bonds continued the trading post in Ramah, which is now owned by Atheling's son, Edgar Bond.

The cowboy minister, Andrew Vander Wagen, established a Trading Post in Halona Square in Zuni, which is now owned by his granddaughter, Elaine Thomas, and her husband, Roger.

The Crockett families remained on their ranches south of Ramah, running their herds of cattle on the range, but suffered many hardships. Jewel reported recently that her father, Walter Crockett, "lost everything" in the year 1929, but managed to keep the ranches, which he deeded to his sons before his death in 1957. Walter Crockett's wife, Claudia, died in 1951.

Feliz Bustamante, who lived happily with the Millers when she was a child, reports that there was a quarrel "over nothing" between her father-in-law, Solomon Dias, and Isadora. After that the Millers started loading the buckboard. "They left everything," Feliz said. "They just took their personal possessions and supplies and corn for the team. They left all the cattle, horses, chickens—everything, and I never saw them again."

As a parting gift, Isadora gave Feliz a photograph of herself and John Miller which was taken just before they left for Arizona. The Millers were standing in the courtyard under the windmill behind the house, and Isadora's hand was still bandaged where it had been torn by a gopher trap. Isadora was showing the effects of a lifetime of hard work and illness. Her natural attractiveness had been damaged by a lack of dental care and loss of teeth, and a mole, left unattended, had grown on her nose. Also of note, John Miller, for the first time, was not wearing a holster and gun. Miller, too, looked older and was showing the devastating effects of years of struggle and hard work.

The photograph of John and Isadora is now owned by Feliz's son, Herman Bustamante. It is the only known photograph of John and Isadora Miller together, and the only photograph of Isadora known to exist.

In spite of everything, Miller had managed to outlive most of his old enemies.

Pat Garrett had been murdered in 1909, either by a man named Wayne Brazil, or by a hired gunman who, ironically, was called Killer Miller.

Governors Axtell and Wallace were both dead. The Murphy-Dolan Gang and the Santa Fe Ring were history.

Old Timers in Ramah remember the morning the Millers drove through town heading south. Their buckboard was loaded high with their possessions, and the people of Ramah stood at the side of the road and waved good-bye, and some of them wept. It is always sad to lose a good neighbor. After the departure of the Millers, Don Silvestre Mirabel leased the Miller Place to Arza Nicoll and his wife Clara. They moved into the Miller Place with seven of their children who were still at home, so that the children could attend the one-room school on the Crockett Ranch, which was still taught by Kate Sanders, niece of Walter Crockett. The Nicolls' son, W. W. Nicolls, who now lives in Bosque Farms, New Mexico, was interviewed in September, 1989. W.W. Nicolls said that John Miller added a series of rooms to the original two main rooms, without connecting doors and no windows. Apparently the extra rooms had been occupied by various people, including outlaws, who often stayed at the Miller place.

W.W. Nicolls, who was about twelve years of age when the Nicolls family moved into the Miller home, remembers seeing John Miller and his wife, Isadora, in McGaffey just before the Millers left New Mexico. People were pointing out an old couple sitting in a buckboard. "That's John Miller, and his wife," they were saying. Young Nicoll wondered what was so unusual about an old man and an old woman in a buckboard. It was not until years later that he understood they were pointing out John Miller because they thought he was Billy the Kid. The Millers were in McGaffey for a final visit with Miller's old friend, Herman Tecklenburg, before they left for Arizona.

After the departure of the Nicolls family, the house that John Miller built with his own two hands was torn down. It was just another old house that had outlived its usefulness. Only the cedar-lined well with the foul tasting water remains. But Miller Canyon and the beautiful Miller Forest are still there. And one day perhaps another fugitive from bureaucratic injustice, or a refugee from a teeming city jungle will find a sanctuary there.

Once again perhaps children will play on the soft pine needle floor of the Miller Forest beneath the tall pines, and will shake sweet tasting nuts from the cones of the pinon trees, and will startle the deer and birds, and try to catch the squirrels and chipmunks. And maybe one day another little boy will tie a line on a pole, bait a hook with a worm, and catch a bright and shiny trout in the Rio Pescado.

Perhaps the little boy will be one of the many descendants of Max Miller, and he will say to his wide-eyed playmates: "My Great granddaddy used to live here, and his Daddy was Billy the Kid."

John and Isadora Miller: This photograph of the Millers was taken just before they left the Miller Ranch for Arizona where they hoped to regain their health. Miller was suffering from rheumatism, and Isadora was losing her sight, and was showing the results of years of hard work and a lack of medical and dental care.
Miller, for the first time, is shown without a gun. Isadora still has her hand bandaged from wounds received when her hand was caught in a gopher trap.
©, Herman Bustamante, 1990.

Don Silvestre Mirabel's home in San Rafael as it is today.

W. W. Nichols: Nichol's family moved into the John Miller home when John and Isadora left for Arizona. W.W. Nichols lives in Los Lunas, NM.

—15—

Arizona Bound

W hen the Millers left the village of Ramah, they headed towards El Morro, where they turned south for the long trip over hazardous mountain roads with their loaded buckboard and team of horses. They must have remembered another time, some thirty-seven years earlier, when, as a young couple, they had driven a loaded buckboard out of Las Vegas to El Morro and the beginning of a new life in the western part of the Territory. Now, much older, they were headed back to El Morro en route to Arizona, where they would start a new life in another state where the weather was warm and the prospects bright.

The friends John and Isadora Miller left behind in the Zuni Mountain area may have thought the Millers had slipped away to die, but John Miller was not one to accept defeat easily, and he certainly was not ready to die—not yet. Calling upon the courage, determination, and never failing optimism that had brought them through many years of strife and danger, John and Isadora knew they would succeed again. John Miller, like an old boot, was weathered and worn, but still tough.

The Millers made their way to the village of San Simon, west of El Paso, near the Mexican border in Arizona, where they lived for some two years, and where they were visited by their son, Max, when he returned from the war after his parents had thought him dead.

The border towns between Arizona and Mexico and the surrounding farms and military establishments were familiar territory to John Miller, who many years before, when he was a teenager known as Henry McCarty, worked on the farms and ranches there, courted the Mexican señoritas, learned to speak Spanish, and played monte at the gaming tables. The Chisum Brothers owned the Eureka Springs Stock ranch some twenty miles from Fort Grant at that time, which may have been one of the ranches where young Henry McCarty was employed, and may have been where he first became acquainted with the rancher, John Chisum, who played such an important role later in his life in Lincoln County. It was also on the Mexican border that Henry McCarty first got into serious trouble with the law when he shot and killed a man named F.P. "Windy" Cahill, who had been badgering him in a border saloon in the village of Bonito.

Researcher Bob Barron reports: "It is a known fact that the Kid worked at the Sierra Bonita Ranch, about ten miles from Camp Grant during that time. William Whelan, the foreman, remembered him and testified so. The Kid also spent time in San Simon and other places in this area."

Sometime in the year 1920, the Millers left San Simon and moved to Buckeye, Arizona, because of the hot mineral springs there, which Miller hoped would help his arthritic condition.

According to Robert Barron of El Paso, who researched the life of John Miller in Arizona, Miller soon established himself as a farmer and horse trainer in Buckeye, where he worked at various times on farms owned by the brothers, Ross Conley and Ellis Conley.

The Millers lived for a time on the Ellis Conley Ranch. Later Miller built his own house in Liberty, a settlement near Buckeye, some two hundred yards from the home of Joe Baxter, who was raising a family of motherless children. Joe's wife, Margaret, died in 1928, leaving a little girl and three boys for her widowed husband to raise.

Carl Baxter, the eldest son, who is now sixty-eight years of age, still lives in Buckeye and was interviewed on November 1, 1990.

Carl Baxter remembers John Miller as a kind man who "took me and my younger brother under his wing to help us and teach us how to do things no one else knew how to do.

"Miller taught me how to train a horse to lie down so I could reach the saddle to tie on a load," Baxter said. "And he taught me how to make a balky mule go by turning a mouse loose in its ear. After that, all you had to do was walk up to the mule with your hand in your pocket, and the mule would never balk again."

Baxter called Miller Old Dad. "Old Dad and I worked together," he said. "I didn't have a mother, and Old Dad showed me the way to go. We were buddies. We did things together, and he helped me get work. When we were hauling he would say 'Give 'em to the Kid.'

"Miller knew how to get whatever he needed, and he helped other people, too. He knew when we needed something, and he would get it to us somehow.

"Miller liked to soak in the ditch to keep cool in summer," Baxter remembered. "And one time the irrigation company shut off the water in the ditch and installed a head gate upstream. So Miller drilled holes in the head gate, and the water kept coming."

Baxter remembers that Miller liked to show off his prowess with a pistol. "He would stick a turkey feather in a post. Then he'd step off forty steps, turn, and trim one side off the turkey feather, and then the other side, and leave the stem standing there."

Baxter recalled that one time he brought a book about Billy the Kid home from the library and was reading it to John Miller. "Miller at times would become very angry at something that was written about the Kid," Baxter said. Miller would say: "That's a damn lie. They don't even know where the corral was."

When the Miller house caught fire, young Carl Baxter helped carry Isadora's body from the burning building. "She was a corpse," Baxter said, "but she wasn't burned." Baxter thinks she may have died before the fire started. Her body, Baxter thinks, was probably buried in the Old Cemetery in Buckeye.

Carl Baxter vividly remembers an old humpbacked oval trunk that Miller kept next to the fireplace, covered with an Indian blanket. "You had to be very close to Miller to get near that trunk," Baxter said. "Miller kept his guns in there, and some photographs, keepsakes and papers. He showed me a pistol with twenty-one notches, some ammunition, old cartridges, a buffalo gun, pictures, and a slug he dug out of his body with a pocket knife. And he showed me a ceramic jar with a lid on it that he kept in the bottom of the trunk that was filled with gold and silver coins.

"After the fire," Baxter said, "I was helping to clean out the burned building, and we found a patch of melted gold coins on the floor where the old trunk stood—about half of a teacup full of melted gold."

Baxter does not know what happened to the trunk, the guns it held, or the rest of the coins and keepsakes. So far as Baxter knows, Miller did not save any possessions from the fire. "All he had was a pair of trousers made from flour sacks," Baxter said.

But Baxter remembered that the night before the fire, Miller had been up all night wandering about. It is probable that the trunk was hidden and retrieved by Miller, and when he died someone found it and turned it over to the court authorities in Phoenix. A representative of the court may have then taken the trunk to Ramah, where Eugene Lambson reported a representative of the Phoenix court walked into his (Lambson's) sandwich shop and asked if Lambson could direct him to an heir to John Miller's estate. The court representative said the trunk contained papers and photographs that proved John Miller was Billy the Kid.

Obviously, up until the fire, Miller had saved some of the coins that the Canadian police officer, Frank Creasy, reported Miller had stolen when he participated in a bank robbery in Montana in 1909.

Like other people who were caught up in the great depression of the 1930's, the Baxters were desperately poor, and Carl Baxter remembers that when Miller knew they were hungry, he would bring them eggs, which Baxter suspected Miller may have stolen from someone else.

Once again, the Robin Hood characteristic of John Miller became evident—reminiscent of the times when, as a young outlaw cowboy known as Billy the Kid, he would slaughter a maverick and would ride through the night distributing the meat to poor people around Fort Sumner. Then, as a rancher in western New Mexico, he would often slaughter a steer and would ride all night through the wilderness areas delivering meat to starving families in the Ramah-Zuni mountains. Miller had his own home grown "share the wealth" philosophy, which he followed throughout his life on behalf of the deserving poor.

Ethel Conley, now ninety-one, wife of the late Ellis Conley, still lives in Buckeye, and was recently interviewed by Robert Barron. Mrs. Conley said she and her husband were fond of the Millers and especially liked John Miller, who they referred to as Dad Miller. Mrs. Conley said that in fifty years of farming and raising horses, John Miller was the best horseman they had ever known.

"He was a good worker," Mrs. Conley said. "If he said he would be here at 6:00 A.M., he was here at 6:00 A.M."

Shortly after their arrival in Buckeye, the Millers took a nine year old orphan boy, Ted O'Brien, into their home to raise. When he was grown, Ted married a local girl, Eulah Burnett, and moved to California, where it is reported he died in 1988. Ethel Conley said that the Millers were kind to Ted, but were strict with him, and saw to it that he attended school and received an education. But Ted was not happy living with the Millers, and soon drifted away, working for a time at the Conley ranch, before he married and moved to California.

"Mrs. Miller was a compassionate woman, who was meticulously clean," Mrs. Conley reported, "but she was in poor health. She was thin, and had a mole on her nose, which may have been cancerous, and may have been the actual cause of her death."

Mrs. Conley remembers Isadora sitting in a rocking chair with a loaded pistol on the table at her side. "Mrs. Miller was almost blind," Mrs. Conley said, "but she was still sewing on clothes she was making for her husband, John Miller."

In a later interview in October, 1990, Ethel Conley remembered more details of the years John Miller worked for Ethel and her husband, Ellis: "John Miller worked for us for three years," she said. "During that time John Miller talked about Billy the Kid often. We thought he had been a companion of Billy the Kid and was hiding because he had been stealing horses and the law was after him.

"Miller said he and some others had a ranch in a canyon where they hid their stolen horses until they could sell them. The horses were hidden from view in a brush-covered corral."

Presumably the ranch in the canyon to which Miller referred was the ranch at Portales which Miller, who was then known as Billy the Kid, owned in partnership with Charles Bowdre.

Ethel Conley also recalled an intriguing incident John Miller told her about his early relationship with his wife, Isadora, in Fort Sumner: "Miller was visiting Isadora at her home in Fort Sumner one evening when someone rushed into the house to warn him that officers were coming to capture him. Miller ran out the back door, where five riders who were friends were waiting with a saddled horse for Miller. Miller said he was shot in the shoulder and knee, and when he came back, Isadora took care of him. Miller said he then told Isadora: "You can throw your shoes under my bed from now on."

Ethel Conley said that Miller showed the bullet scars in his shoulder and knee to her and her husband to prove his story.

Ethel Conley and her husband Ellis had a great liking for John Miller who, Ethel said, was the best man with horses that they had ever known. "He could look a horse in the eye and tell its nature—if it was a spirited animal that would be hard to handle, or if it would be gentle and dependable, and could be used to help train the other horses."

The Conley farm in Buckeye was a vast spread of flat fields covered with Bermuda grass with roots that grew deep. To plow the fields, John

Miller would hook up eight or twelve horses, four abreast, to pull the big plows. Sometimes it was blazing hot, and the inside horses had to be rotated with the outside horses to safeguard them from heat exhaustion.

"One time," Ethel recalled, "the horses bolted, and Old Dad braced his feet, held on to the reins, and guided the horses around and around the field until they wore themselves out."

The Conleys found Miller to be completely trustworthy. "He never stole a thing," Ethel said, "and he never told a lie. We would go off and leave the Millers in charge of the house and stock with complete confidence. They were very honest people. If needed, Miller would come to work at two o'clock in the morning.

"When I returned from the hospital with my newborn daughter, Georgie, Isadora picked her up and kissed her. It was Georgie's first kiss."

Ethel Conley vividly remembered that the Millers owned a big old trunk which stood in the kitchen, and seemed to be their most treasured possession. "They kept it locked," Ethel reported, "but Isadora would open it to put her ivory handled pistol, which was her pride and joy, safely inside. The Millers took the trunk wherever they moved. It was the only piece of furniture they kept with them when they moved."

According to others who knew them, the old trunk was also used by the Millers to store Miller's guns and other treasures.

Georgie Jackson, daughter of Ellis and Ethel Conley, who lives in Phoenix, Arizona, and who as a child, knew Isadora and John Miller well, does not believe that John Miller was Billy the Kid. Mrs. Jackson, like others in the Buckeye community, apparently did not know that Miller lived for over thirty-five years in the Ramah-Zuni wilderness area of New Mexico, where he raised and trained fine horses and operated a cattle ranch. It is a puzzle that Miller did not reveal this fact to the people in the Buckeye area. Perhaps he was still hiding his identity, even from his friends. Miller had been through the nightmare of having to face the possibility of hanging by a rope until dead, and he wanted no more of it.

Georgie Jackson writes: "He (Miller) was on the run with his wife. I don't remember her name as Isadora because he always called her 'Eeh Haw' which was a Comanche name for 'my love.'

"He (Miller) told us his mother was a Comanche Indian, and his father was a white man. He said he never had a pair of pants until he was seven years old. He lived in Texas with his mother and the Comanche Indians until he was grown. They taught him how to steal horses and use them. My father always said he was the best with horses he had ever seen.

"Miller called Ellis Conley 'Essie.' Miller would say: 'Essie, Billy the Kid is no good, no good.'"

Georgie Jackson continued: "Miller knew Billy the Kid and ran with him on some of his escapades. John Miller told us he had a horse stealing corral in a canyon in New Mexico. Most of John Miller's doings were horse stealing. He was taught by the Comanche Indians. He lived with them. He grew up there, not New York."

Nellie Dixon, daughter of the Ross Conleys, remembers that John Miller often came to the Conley home to listen to a weekly radio program about Billy the Kid. "Sometimes when he thought the program was wrong, he would complain and shake his fist," Nellie said. "But when he liked what he heard, he would laugh and clap his hands."

Bob Barron also interviewed Joe Conley, son of Ross Conley. Joe Conley, who is now seventy-one years of age, said he remembers John Miller very well. Conley attended school with Ted O'Brien.

Joe Conley said that John Miller was a good and dependable worker, but he was dodging the law. Joe Conley's father, Ross Conley, always cut Miller's hair because Miller thought there were posters out for his arrest with his description, and he was wary of going to the barber in town because he thought someone might recognize him from the wounds on his body.

Throughout his long life, Miller delighted in showing off his pistol shooting skills to admiring friends. Joe Conley said his father, Ross Conley, remembered seeing Miller trim the sides off a turkey feather with his pistol, one side at a time. Miller was popular with the children in the Buckeye/Liberty community and would show off his gun tricks to amuse them, just as he had formerly entertained people in Lincoln County and the Zuni Mountain area with his fabulous pistol feats.

Miller performed another stunt that must have had special significance for him because of the memories it held in connection with his escape from death by hanging in Lincoln County. Miller would ask the children in Buckeye to tie his wrists together with a rope, "as tight as you can." Then Miller would slip his hands out of the knot and would laugh and say, "Billy the Kid could do that."

When Miller was living in the Ramah-Zuni mountain areas of New Mexico, he often asked people there to help him perform this trick, and when he had freed himself, he always said, "Billy the Kid could do that."

Miller must have been very grateful for a kind Providence that gave him small hands and large wrists which enabled him to free himself from handcuffs and escape from jail several times, and actually saved his life when he freed himself and escaped from the Lincoln County jail.

Demonstrating this trick was a subtle method Miller used to let people know that he was Billy the Kid without actually telling them he was. Miller knew that very few people could free themselves from a tight rope tied about their wrists. In his heart, he probably hoped that some of the people who watched him do it, would put two and two together and would know John Miller's secret—that he really was Billy the Kid.

Joe Conley said that Miller drank a lot at times, and he smoked a pipe filled with tobacco he mixed himself, with a special tobacco he ordered from Tennessee. "It was the worst tobacco I had ever smelled," Conley said.

Conley always thought the old man was hiding something. "Miller," he said, "was very critical of stories appearing in various publications those days about Billy the Kid. Miller said that they were "wrong. . . all wrong, and I ought to know because I was there."

What John Miller did not know was that Billy the Kid had already become a mythical character—a young man of many faces, created by writers, movie makers, and even historians who found in Billy the Kid an intriguing youth about whom they could invent tales as wild, exciting, and sensational as their imaginations could conceive. Because Miller could not reveal his identity, he could only protest to himself. The few people around who watched him shake his fist and exclaim in frustration were puzzled by his obvious outrage over the character assassination of the young man who was known as Billy the Kid.

Conley said that Miller did not elaborate too much on stories of his experiences in New Mexico, but sometimes, when he was in his cups he would tell stories of stealing horses, and once told of raiding a town. (Presumably these events occurred when Miller was an outlaw in Lincoln County, where he was known as Billy the Kid.)

"Miller," Conley said, "often described Billy the Kid physically, as we know John Miller now, including the two protruding front teeth."

John Miller's sense of humor never deserted him, and when speaking of Billy the Kid, he often used a subterfuge to cover his identity with joking remarks. Sometimes he would say: "Billy the Kid often put his boots under our bed," or "the Kid often stayed at my house."

Miller was also still spreading confusion about his identity. When people in Buckeye asked about his heritage, he replied: "My mother was a Comanche Indian and my father was a no-good buffalo hunter."

When the Millers lived in the Ramah-Zuni area, they had the following reply for any curious questioners who asked where they came from: "We escaped from a carnival in Gallup."

Miller said "he knew Billy the Kid," and once, when asked if he knew John Chisum, Miller replied: "Yes, I worked for the Chisum Brothers." (Researchers point out that few people knew that Chisum had brothers who helped in the operation of the Chisum Ranches.)

Miller claimed to have owned the gun that belonged to Billy the Kid, but said that he gave it to his son, Max Miller, when Max visited him in Buckeye. He never explained to anyone how he came by the gun. Miller owned two other guns that he kept in a trunk, but he did not give any history of them that is remembered by anyone in Buckeye, and no one knows what happened to them. (Another gun owned by Miller was given to a cowpuncher, Frank Burrard Creasy, who worked for Miller on his ranch near Pescado, New Mexico. The gun was treasured by Creasy as Billy the Kid's gun, and is now owned by Creasy's heirs in Ontario, Canada, where Creasy was a famous police inspector.)

After the death of Isadora, Miller failed rapidly, both physically and mentally, and according to his son, Max, fell off a roof he was repairing and was badly injured.

When Miller could no longer take care of himself, he was driven to the mountain village of Prescott, Arizona, by his friend, Ross Conley, where he was admitted into the Pioneer Home there on March 12, 1937. Miller was unhappy about leaving his home in Buckeye, but nevertheless he could still joke. When asked when he came to live in Arizona, he replied: "Right after the capture of Geronimo."

During the last months of Miller's life, he tried to get someone to come see him at Prescott, indicating that he wanted to set the record straight about his life as an outlaw. Several times he had told friends that he would tell them the truth about himself before he died. In this effort, he contacted Ellis Conley, who was ill at the time, and could not come. He then contacted Ross Conley who was not able to make the trip to Prescott. He also wrote to his son, Max, asking him to come "take me home," but Max could not make it in time, either.

For Miller it was too late. His story, which he meant to have officially recorded, was not so done, and the saga of John Miller, alias Billy the Kid, was left to historians to debate, reconstruct, and ponder.

True, Miller had told his son, Max, and some close friends that he was Billy the Kid, but they were all honor bound not to reveal the information until after Miller's death. Also, Max, like his Dad, shunned publicity. He was a quiet and modest man, and he did not attach great importance to the fact that his Dad was Billy the Kid.

Without exception, all of the people to whom Miller confided that he was Billy the Kid, respected his wishes and kept the promise not to reveal his identity until after his death. Since Miller's death, various people have tried to tell their stories, but no one would listen. The myths surrounding Billy the Kid and Pat Garrett were too overwhelming, and one by one, the testimonies that Billy the Kid had escaped death at Fort Sumner, were silenced.

There is no evidence that John Miller told anyone in Buckeye that he had lived for over thirty years in the Ramah-Zuni wilderness area of New Mexico. This is strange, indeed, unless before he left New Mexico for Arizona, Miller had reason to believe that the authorities in Santa Fe had traced him to the Ramah-Zuni area. Once again he was burning bridges behind him and was covering his tracks—once again fleeing for his life.

The Old Timers in the Buckeye/Liberty area in Arizona who knew John Miller in his later years all believed Miller had some connection with Billy the Kid, but apparently he did not tell anyone that he actually was the Kid.

Carl Baxter, who was John Miller's closest neighbor, said: "I believe that John Miller knew Billy the Kid."

Ethel Conley is inclined to believe that Miller could have been the Kid. It was, however, difficult for many people to reconcile the kind man who was John Miller, with the outlaw image they held of Billy the Kid. Mrs. Conley's daughter, Georgie Jackson said: "I would have trusted my life to John Miller."

Joe Conley does not think John Miller was the Kid, but says Miller must have had some connection with the Kid.

Billy the Kid was the only member of the Regulator Gang who was not pardoned by Governor Wallace at the end of the Lincoln County War. Therefore, Billy the Kid was the only member of the group who was forced to live the rest of his life as a fugitive, hiding from the law. And Billy the Kid was the only member of the Regulator Group who was wanted for killing two guards when he escaped from the Lincoln County jail.

John Miller in his youth was known throughout the world as the brave young man who was called Billy the Kid, and who, in a bloody war known as The Lincoln County War, heroically took on the corrupt Santa Fe Ring conspiracy which murdered and stole, and exerted dictatorial power over the economy and political life of the Territory of New Mexico. Billy the Kid has been the subject of some eight hundred articles and books and dozens of movies and T.V. documentaries. Many people made great sums of money from the lurid tales they told of the exploits of Billy the Kid. But John Miller, because he was always hiding from the law, benefitted from none of it—a bitter pill it must have been for a man who was always struggling against poverty, and was always faced with the likelihood that if he became too conspicuous, he would alert members of the Santa Fe Ring, who would send killers to assassinate him, or would capture and hang him.

John Miller died at the Pioneer Home in Prescott, Arizona, on November 7, 1937, at six-thirty in the evening.

And so William Bonney, alias Billy the Kid, alias John Miller, alias The Old Man, alias Old Dad, died alone and was buried in the Pioneer Home Cemetery in Prescott. But John Miller won the last round. He was not hanged by lackeys of the Santa Fe Ring.

John Miller left behind friends who grieved for him in Buckeye, and from all over the West, through Texas, Arizona, and New Mexico to El Paso, Silver City, the Mogollon Mountains and Reserve, to Fort Sumner and Lincoln and across the state of New Mexico to Ramah and Zuni.

Any interested person who may be in the vicinity of the historic mountain village of Prescott, Arizona, might like to visit the Pioneer Home Cemetery where the name "John Miller" is inscribed on a memorial plaque along with the names of his fellow pioneers who died there during the years from 1914 to 1938.

Robert Barron, with the help of Gary Abbate, Director of Resident Services at the Pioneer Home in Prescott, located the Memorial and grave site of John Miller.

It is appropriate that John Miller, one of the Old West's most famous pioneers, is buried there at the Pioneer Home Cemetery, where he is honored as one of the brave frontiersmen who carved a civilization out of the old Western Frontier.

Memorial Plaque at Pioneer Cemetery in Prescott, Arizona, where John Miller is listed as one of the pioneers who is buried there.

Close-up of above plaque.

Ross Conley, Arizona rancher, on whose ranch John Miller worked and lived.

Joe Conley, son of
Ross Conley.

Nellie Conley Dixon (l) & Ruby Conley Page (r)
Daughters of Ross Conley. Photo by Bob Barron

Ellis Conley, friend and employer of John Miller, in front of his home in Buckeye, Arizona.

Ethel Conley, widow of Ellis Conley on whose farm Miller was employed during his late years in Buckeye, Arizona. Ethel Conley lives in Buckeye at the present time.

Researcher Robert Barron

Arizona Pioneer Home in Prescott, Arizona where John Miller spent his last days.

—16—

Max Miller and Bill Crockett

In the year 1919, after his discharge from the army, Max Miller returned home and found the homestead abandoned, and his parents gone. He had no place to stay so he returned to live with the Crockett family. Max said he had hitchhiked home after his discharge from the army and was heartbroken to find his parents gone. He knew nothing about the notification his Dad had received from the army that he was missing in action and presumed dead.

Max was joyfully welcomed by the Crocketts. He was a brother who had returned after they had thought him dead. The Crockett girls were especially delighted because, they said, "he looked so handsome in his military uniform."

When Max Miller was interviewed in 1976, he told about his return from the army: "When I came back from Germany, I couldn't find the Old Man. Lou Shoemaker said he was in Phoenix. Shoemaker wrote the Old Man a letter, and the Old Man wrote back and told me how to get there. A friendly man took me over there. My mother was very old and couldn't see much. I stayed six months or more cutting hay, but it was too hot, and I came back to New Mexico."

Max said he found his parents living in a two-room adobe house on an acreage at San Simon. John and Isadora raised some chickens, planted a garden, and John Miller worked for a man named John Shaw, who owned a farm nearby.

After visiting his parents at San Simon and after again visiting them when they had moved to Buckeye, Max complained that his parents spent too much time soaking in the ditches to keep cool in the summer and in the hot springs to ease aching joints in the winter. The young man had other ideas of how to spend his time, and returned to a more familiar area and went to work for Adrian Berryhill in the Zuni Mountains, where he obtained a job riding herd on the range. Berryhill owned two large ranches with headquarters at Ambrosia Lake, north of Grants, and Max lived alone in a tent, riding the range to protect the herd of some six hundred cattle. Joe Tietjen, a nephew of Adrian Berryhill, delivered groceries to Max and checked to see that he was all right. Joe remembers that Max always kept a saddled horse ready to ride out in case of trouble, and he was always out of tobacco. It was not an easy life, and a lonely one, but it was the life that Max knew and loved.

Joe Tietjen lives in Bosque Farms, New Mexico, and in a recent interview related fond memories of the five years he worked with Max Miller. "Max was quiet," he said. "He didn't talk much, but he was a good cowpuncher."

After the death of John Miller, Tietjen said Max would have a drink or two and would loosen up a little and would laugh and say: "I'm a tough Navajo. My Dad was Billy the Kid."

Joe Tietjen and others who knew Max report that Max told them his Dad, John Miller, made him promise that he would not reveal the fact that Miller was Billy the Kid until after his death. Max kept the promise.

Max Miller was a man of few words who had a way of condensing whole lifetimes into a couple of short paragraphs, period. Max sadly and briefly reported the tragedies that struck his parents after he had returned to New Mexico from his last visit with them:

"My parents moved to Buckeye, Arizona, because the Old Man said there were hot springs there that would help his rheumatism. My mother smoked cigarettes, and was smoking in bed and set the house on fire, and died. Then the Old Man was by himself. I wrote and told him to come back home, but he wouldn't do it. Then he fell off a roof he was fixing and was hurt, and he wrote and told me to come bring him home. But it was too late. I didn't have any money, and he died before I could get down there."

Max Miller lived with the Crocketts until he left to marry a Navajo woman, Irene Adekaih. He later married another Navajo woman, Alice, and lived for the rest of his life at Borrego Pass, where he raised sheep and cattle. Whenever possible, he visited his younger "brother" Bill Crockett, who owned a bar and a ranch on the highway to Fence Lake between the Zuni and Navajo Reservations.

All through the years a close relationship existed between Max Miller and Bill Crockett, who was a baby when Max returned from the war.

Bill Crockett inherited his parents' musical talents, and his cowboy bar at the edge of the Zuni wilderness was not only an oasis where people met to drown their sorrows and celebrate their joys, but it was also a place where they could dance to the riotous rhythms of what can best be described as "Indian Rock." It was Bill Crockett's band, equipped with the most modern electronic instruments and sound effects. Crockett was director, vocalist, and lyricist, and it was quite a band. Bill Crockett, rancher, cowboy, barkeeper and director of the band, wrote this account of his friend Max Miller, and of Max's father, "The Old Man":

"I am writing this to the best of my belief and what I have been told by others. I do believe John Miller was truly William Bonney, alias Billy the Kid. He had a Mexican wife, and lived in caves in the area, not staying in any cave for too long. Later he homesteaded 160 acres which was all the government allowed at that time. The area is still known as Miller Canyon, next to Forest Service land, which was later given to the Zuni Indian Tribe. Some time after moving to Miller Canyon, Miller and his wife adopted a Navajo Indian baby, who was of the Skeet family. He named the baby Max Miller, who turned out to be a life-long friend of mine.

"John Miller was certainly a respected man in the area. Everyone liked him. As far as I know he never harmed anyone there. Every time Miller bought a new hat, he always sewed the brim of the old one on to the new one. I never did know why. Miller moved to Buckeye, Arizona, and I always wondered about that. I made a trip to Buckeye and near there was an old mineral bath, and hotel, and I figured he went there for the mineral baths, as all those years of horseback riding had taken their toll on Miller. He was probably looking for something to take the stiffness and rheumatism from his body, kind of a Fountain of Youth deal.

"Max told me many times that Miller had told him about the Lincoln County War and Pat Garrett, who Miller said was his good friend. Miller said there was a Mexican shot and buried in the coffin that was supposed to be the Kid.

"Max Miller was not known by the Navajo Indians as Max Miller; they all called him Billy the Kid's Son. In Max's later years he became deaf and was awful hard to communicate with. However, he spoke five languages, which was a credit to him.

"Before I left New Mexico, I went and got Max to stay with me for a while, as he was like a brother to me. At the time I was running a bar, and Max liked to go in the bar and visit with some of his old friends. I had told the bartenders to take special care of him and to give him anything he wanted. This was supposed to be his last day there, as he was ready to go home, so he over-celebrated and the bartender brought him into the house with a big knot on his forehead, sticking out about two inches, and Max said, 'I can't go home looking like this.'

"The bartender said he had fallen and hit his head on the corner of the bar. Next morning it was worse and had turned blue and he was worrying about going home like that. I told one of my bartenders to take him to the Zuni P.H.S. Hospital and see if they could drain some of the blood from the knot, so it would go down, as he was ready to go home.

"The bartender took him to the hospital and presented him to the receptionist. She asked his name and what tribe of Indian he was, Navajo or Zuni.

"Max said: "My mother was a Mexican. My Dad was a white man, who was Billy the Kid. My brother is Bill Crockett who runs a bar a few miles from here."

"The receptionist said to go ahead and take him to the doctor, but what he really needs is to see a psychiatrist. That knot on his head has got him really confused.

"Max stayed with me another ten days, and I was glad to have his company. He was like a brother to me, so faithful, honest, and true.

"Max passed on recently at the age of ninety-four. I hold fond memories of him. I pray the Good Lord will hold him gently in the palm of His hand. The best cowboy I ever had the pleasure of riding with."

MAX MILLER

The guns of World War I
Tore at his eardrums
As his Platoon
Marched through the Land of France
And he breathed
The German's mustard gas.
Everywhere there was the stench
Of flesh decaying
While blood ran down the trenches,
And no man knew
Who would be the next to die.
Yet Max endured it all
And still came marching home.
With medals for his bravery
He was bestowed-
This young man who was a Navajo.
And now we pay our last respects
To our adopted brother, Max,
With his sense of humor and dignity
And a twinkle in his eye
Because he loved the Land he fought for
He was not afraid to die.

(By Jewel Crockett Lambson, 1988)

Joe Tietjen, friend of Max Miller.
Tietjen lives in Los Lunas, NM.

Max Miller in his late eighties when he was interviewed a few years before his death.

Bill Crockett: Bill's family owned the ranch that adjoined the Miller homestead. Bill was a lifelong friend of John and Isadora's adopted son, Max Miller.

Afterword

There are still questions about that night in Fort Sumner. Perhaps there always will be.

Some people will always believe that Pat Garrett shot and killed Billy the Kid in Pete Maxwell's house on July 14, 1881. Some people will believe that Billy the Kid was buried the next morning in the cemetery at Fort Sumner alongside his pals Tom O'Folliard and Charles Bowdre.

People will still believe what they will even if scientific facts and research prove that the Kid was not killed that night, but lived a long life as a rancher in the Ramah-Zuni mountains of New Mexico, and was known as John Miller.

New questions, however, arise. If Pat Garrett did not shoot Billy the Kid that night, who did he shoot? Or, was an empty casket buried the next morning as some people think?

Why has the casket in the cemetery at Fort Sumner, which supposedly contains the remains of Billy the Kid, not been exhumed to determine once and for all if the Kid was actually buried there, or if someone was buried in his stead, or if the casket is empty? There are scientific experts like Clyde Snow, who determined the validity of the Nazi Joseph Mengele's death by a study of the bones in his casket, who could give a valid answer to whether or not the Kid was buried at Fort Sumner.

If an honest study of all the evidence proves that John Miller was indeed Billy the Kid, there are still unanswered questions.

Where did John and Isadora Miller obtain a sturdy buckboard loaded with provisions, a fine team of horses, a well-bred saddle horse and seven head of cattle which their son, Max Miller, said his Dad told him they had?

Billy the Kid was a penniless cowboy hiding from the law, living precariously from day to day. There was no way he could have put together such an impressive supply of goods and equipment.

Was the Kid's benefactor the Cattle Queen of the Pecos, Susan McSween, as some people have said? Did Susan McSween obtain funds from John Tunstall's family in England to furnish Billy the Kid and his wife with supplies to enable them to start life anew in inhospitable country? Was the Tunstalls' generosity a show of gratitude for Billy's loyalty to their son, whose murder set off the Lincoln County War?

Who did John and Isadora Miller visit during their yearly trips to El Paso for provisions?

If John and Isadora went to El Paso each year as has been reported by several people who knew them, Miller was certainly taking a chance on his life, because Pat Garrett lived there then. Garrett was appointed Sheriff of Dona Ana County for two terms by Governor W.W. Thornton of New Mexico and, in the year 1901, was appointed Collector of Customs at El Paso by President Theodore Roosevelt. Later, he settled in Las Cruces just over the border from El Paso.

Could it have been possible that John and Isadora went to El Paso specifically to visit Miller's old friend, Pat Garrett? And along the way, did they perhaps visit with Billy's stepfather, William Antrim, who lived in Mogollon?

Or perhaps it was as the Millers said. They went to El Paso for supplies.

There is an indication that Billy the Kid was not even at Pete Maxwell's house the night of July 14, 1881, when he was supposed to have been killed there by Pat Garrett. Max Miller said that his Dad, John Miller, told him he was wounded some days before that day, and Max's mother, Isadora, said she took the wounded Kid to her house in Fort Sumner, doctored his wounds, and hid him under the bed between two straw mattresses when officers came looking for him. "Officers," meaning Pat Garrett and his deputies, conceivably may have been looking for the Kid some days before the shoot-out at Pete Maxwell's house. But after Pat had told everyone he had shot the Kid and buried him in the Fort Sumner cemetery, he surely was not anxious to have it known that the Kid wasn't killed after all, but was hiding at Isadora's house.

Someplace there is a trunk, or the contents of a trunk that authorities from the County Clerk's Office in Arizona found when they disposed of Miller's possessions after his death. The trunk contained letters and documents that belonged to Billy the Kid. The authorities in Phoenix sent a man to Ramah to search for an heir to John Miller's estate. But Max Miller, who was the legal heir, was interviewed in 1978, and said he knew nothing about what happened to the trunk, and was not interested in searching for it. What became of the trunk that contained Billy the Kid's letters and documents? Has it been destroyed by state or county officials in Phoenix or by relatives of Max Miller, the only known heirs to the Miller estate? Or is the trunk and its contents in storage somewhere?

Is there truth to the statement of the Canadian, Frank Creasy, that John Miller was involved in a bank robbery in Montana and was pardoned for a $4,000 fee? Where did the gold coins that Frank Creasy said John Miller had buried out in the forest come from? Were they loot from the bank robbery, or were they part of the package of provisions that Miller received before he left Las Vegas to seek a new life in a new area?

Who was Isadora? Is it possible that Isadora was Charlie Bowdre's widow, Manuela? Certainly there is a resemblance between Isadora and Manuela, noticeable even after thirty-seven years, and even after Isadora had become wrinkled with age, had lost her teeth and had become disfigured by a growth on her nose. Feliz Bustamante, who lived with the Millers and had a close association with Isadora over a period of some ten years, was shown the photograph of Manuela Bowdre. Feliz pointed out that she knew Isadora as an old woman. "However," she said, "there is a similarity."

Manuela and Isadora were tiny women, of Mexican heritage, who spoke Spanish, and never learned to speak English. The great resemblance between the two, however, was their determination to stand side by side with their men, shouldering the responsibility of living with outlaws who were hunted by the law throughout their lives. Isadora, like Manuela, deliberately chose a dangerous and difficult life, and never wavered in times of adversity. Charles Bowdre was fortunate to have a wife like Manuela, and John Miller was fortunate to have a wife like Isadora.

Perhaps one day the photographs of Manuela Bowdre and Isadora Miller will be compared by the modern technology of computer enhancement, and it will be determined if Isadora and Manuela Bowdre were the same person. Then we will know if it was Manuela Bowdre who hid Billy the Kid and tended his wounds at the old hospital building where she and Billy the Kid lived, and where she often offered the hospitality of her home to members of the Regulators when they rode into Fort Sumner.

Deborah Robinson is a sculptress who has been sculpting for twenty-two years. In 1987, she started a wax museum of historical figures of the state of New Mexico. One of the subjects she chose to sculpt was Billy the Kid. Deborah says it took eighteen months to complete the sculpture of the Kid because there were so many contradictory accounts of what he looked like. When the claim that John Miller was Billy the Kid appeared in local newspapers, Deborah decided to compare the two. Here is Deborah's account of how she did it:

"The first step was to figure out Billy's approximate height. I photographed a picture of the tintype of Billy the Kid. Then a tracing was made of a carbine like the one he was holding in the tintype. The negative of the photocopy was projected over the tracing of the gun. Billy measured approximately five feet seven inches tall. The face from the projected figure of Billy the Kid was traced, and the measurements from the tracing were used to complete the sculpture. After the sculpture was finished, the negative from the photocopy was superimposed over the sculpture to check for accuracy.

"During the time I was working on the sculpture of the Kid, an article appeared in the newspaper about a man named John Miller from Ramah, N.M., who was thought to be Billy the Kid. My first reaction to the Miller article was 'not another one.' After studying the photograph in the newspaper for a few minutes, I noticed the hands of John Miller were extremely close to the hands of Billy the Kid—his long thumb, round nails and curved fingers. Studying the face, I noticed the unusual nose, bent to one side, and the buckteeth. I contacted Helen Airy and she sent a photograph of Miller. Miller's photo was photocopied and the negative was projected so that Miller's figure was five feet seven inches tall. Miller's hands, body and facial features were a good match to Billy the Kid. Using one of the finished heads of Billy the Kid, I aged the sculpture to a man of about sixty years, and the resemblance to John Miller was very close. In my opinion, John Miller and Billy the Kid were the same person."

Ann Storrer of Belen writes: "My father, Charlie Walker, grew up around Fort Sumner during the early 1900's. A Mexican he used to work for told him that he saw Billy the Kid at the bullfights in Mexico long after he was supposed to be dead. The rumor around Fort Sumner was that Pat Garrett and Billy the Kid were good friends and Garrett tried to stop everyone from killing Billy. My father believed there was never a body in the grave."

Arleigh Nation of Albuquerque supplied the following story: "A man by the name of Trujillo, who died in 1935 at the age of ninety-five told Nation he worked for Pete Maxwell at the time Billy the Kid was supposed to have been killed. He said the day before the shoot-out they dressed up an Indian, who had died the night before, to look like the Kid. The Indian was buried in the grave that was said to have been the Kid's."

Nation, who is a Billy the Kid buff, also said a neighbor of his who lived in Lincoln, Mrs. Syd Boykin, told him that the Kid stayed at her home in Lincoln many times after he was supposed to have been dead.

Historian Gary Tietjen sent in this story from *Cow Dust and Saddle Leather* (by Ben Kemp with J.C. Dykes. © 1968 by the University of Oklahoma Press). "Ben Kemp's father, Ben, lived around Reserve, then called Milligan Plaza. In 1881, he met Henry Cox and later married Cox's daughter, Josephine. They told him that after leaving Fort Davis they had moved to White Oaks, New Mexico, where they had lived for two years. During this time Henry Cox's daughter Tibitha, married a cowboy by the name of John Collins. Later the family learned that John Collins had been a friend of Billy the Kid. He had warned the Kid against going to Pete Maxwell's house in Fort Sumner on the night of July 14, 1881, when Sheriff Pat Garrett supposedly killed him. Collins claimed that the next day he helped bury the corpse of the man Garrett killed, and it was not Billy the Kid."

Nadine Brady, who owns a bar in Adelino, New Mexico, and whose grandfather was Sheriff William Brady, who was shot by Billy the Kid, was interviewed by Arley Sanches for a story which appeared in the *Albuquerque Journal* on September 8, 1990.

This intriguing item was included in the story: "Nadine says one old timer told her Garrett didn't shoot Bonney. He told her Garrett and Bonney were friends and Garrett invented a story to help his friend escape. A wanderer was killed and buried, and Garrett told everyone he had shot Billy the Kid."

The story that Billy the Kid was not killed by Pat Garrett was not a surprise to Old Timers around Lincoln, many of whom never conceded the Kid's death. Frank Coe, a friend of Billy the Kid during the Lincoln County War, believed to the day of his death that Billy was still alive, and spent a great deal of time tracing reports that he had been seen. Coe once left a home he was investigating with tears in his eyes. He was disappointed because it had been erroneously reported to him that Billy had been there.

In view of the fact that John Miller made frequent trips to El Paso after he was supposedly killed by Pat Garrett, it would be logical to think that there would be Old Timers in the area who would have seen him and identified him as Billy the Kid.

As a matter of fact, there were numerous people around El Paso who did reveal that they had seen Billy the Kid there after the shooting at Fort Sumner. Some reported their stories to the *El Paso Times Herald* and one even revealed information that Billy the Kid was still alive to the New Mexico Historical Society.

El Paso Herald Post, 1926

Billy the Kid, the legendary hero of the Southwest, is the subject of a recent controversy that is interesting all New Mexico. Although he was supposedly shot by Sheriff Pat Garrett over forty years ago and buried in Fort Sumner, at a discussion before the New Mexico Historical Society a few days ago, an El Paso man who withheld his name, sent the statement to the society that "The Kid" was still alive. He knew an old timer who had brought "The Kid" from Texas to New Mexico and who assisted in his escape. The El Paso man met "The Kid" in 1916 in the company of this old friend. A corroboration of the story is told by Manuel Taylor, an old prospector, who used to run races with "The Kid" in Silver City and once pried the bars off the

164

chimney top of the old adobe jail so Billy could climb out. Taylor says he met the Kid in Guadalajara, Mexico, in 1914, and they had a few drinks together. He said "The Kid" had married there and has a family. . . .

El Paso Times Herald, June 29, 1926:

Billy the Kid is alive and resides within a radius of 200 miles of El Paso. He has been in El Paso within the last 10 years and will probably return within the next few months, if a government official here is correct in his statements.

One other person, [a] friend of Billy, is living in El Paso, who says he was present on the night in 1881 when Billy is supposed to have been killed by Pat Garrett, who was then sheriff of Lincoln County, New Mexico.

"When Billy rode away on the county clerk's black mare, after killing his two guards, he rode straight to the home of his sweetheart, Pauline Maxwell, who lived in Fort Sumner," the friend said.

Garrett was Billy's best friend, and therein hangs the tale as told by the friend and the government official who declares Billy is living under an assumed name near El Paso.

FRAMED ESCAPE

"Billy and his friend Garrett framed an escape," the official says."The sheriff had to be away from town that day and he told the guards to watch Billy and not let him escape. Billy escaped, and it was up to Pat Garrett to get him.

"There was a $5,000 reward offered to the captor. Billy was under sentence to hang and wanted to escape.

"The little black mare was swift and Billy easily outdistanced his pursuers. He stayed at the home of his sweetheart that night. Garrett, by prearrangement, went to Paulita's house," the friend said.

This is what Billy's friend says took place that night:

"Billy, here is $1,000; take it and get out of the country as fast as you can," Garrett told Billy. "We will fake a killing and bury some one here tonight so that folks will think I have killed you."

"Pat, I don't need that much money, I will take $25 if you have it. That will be enough to get me far away," Billy told him.

"Billy, I want your solemn promise that you will not carry a gun again for 20 years," said Garrett.

KID RIDES AWAY

"I promise," was Billy's answer.

Both men shook hands over the promise and Billy got on the little black mare and rode into the night.

He is said to have ridden to a man he could trust, a rancher, who would keep his mouth shut and help him. That rancher is still alive and living in El Paso. It is he who tells of the events on that night.

"When Garrett saw Billy vanish into the night, he rushed to the house, fired two shots and with a man who helped him rushed a supposed body from the house before Paulita or any of her family could see it.

"The body was taken to a grave already prepared to receive it without the form of a ceremony. That grave was marked by a rude cross, that was to prove to Billy's sister that he was still alive."

El Paso Times, July 26, 1964

Billy the Kid is dead. There is no doubt about it.

But did he die from the bullets from Sheriff Pat Garrett's gun in July, 1881, or from natural causes in Prescott, Arizona, on Oct. 17, 1955?

The man who reported the above was Leslie Traylor of San Antonio who was a retired Immigration and Naturalization Service inspector. It is interesting but coincidental, that Mr. Traylor traced the man he claimed was Billy the Kid, a man who called himself Henry Street Smith, to his death in Prescott, Arizona. There was certainly no resemblance between the man, Henry Street Smith, and John Miller who was also buried there in 1935.

El Paso Herald Post, June 22, 1926

New Mexico Historical Society has received word from an El Pasoan whose name it has not revealed, but who is said to be a person of prominence, that Billy the Kid is still alive.

It is alleged that Billy, not having been slain at Socorro by Sheriff Pat Garrett, is still alive in some unmentioned place, and the El Pasoan has conversed with him in recent years. He is said to be trying to live down his past.

El Paso Herald Post, 1926

Leland V. Gardiner, local Santa Fe officer, believes "Billie the Kid," notorious outlaw of pioneer days, still lives, and has thought so for the past 10 years, he said.

He is not the El Pasoan, however, who communicated his belief to the New Mexico Historical Society, he declared. That informant said he had seen the Kid about 10 years ago.

"I am not certain, but believe I have seen the Kid," said Mr. Gardiner. `I am told that he is on an isolated ranch within 500 miles of El Paso.

"When strangers come to the ranch, the Kid disappears until the visitors are gone. He was so well known in his day that he can't take chances on being detected.

"One thing that leads me to believe the Kid still lives from what I have read, there was a big standing reward for Billie the Kid, and sheriff Pat Garrett did not collect the reward after he was supposed to have killed the Kid.

"The Kid was not an outlaw by choice. The first killing he committed was forced upon him, and after that he was forced to kill in self-defense."

John Graham (alias John Collins) "claimed he helped bury the corpse of the man Pat Garrett killed and it was not Billy the Kid." University of Oklahoma Press.

168

This is a photograph of a wax sculpture of Billy the Kid, aged to show a remarkable likeness to John Miller.

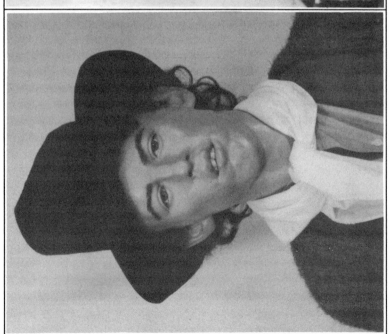

This is a photograph of a wax sculpture of Billy the Kid by sculptress Debbie Robinson.

Sculptress Deborah Robinson of Los Alamos. The sculpture on the previous page and other western sculptures can be viewed in Debbie's wax museum in Santa Fe, NM.

ACKNOWLEDGEMENTS

Ginger Moody: Ginger is the great-granddaughter of that fabulous frontiersman, Herman Tecklenburg. We are grateful to Ginger for the written history she submitted of her great-grandfather and for arranging the interview with her grandfather, John Herman Tecklenburg. Ginger and her husband Ron, and three daughters live in Paradise Hills, a suburb of Albuquerque, New Mexico.

Elaine Thomas: Elaine is the granddaughter of that unforgettable pair, the mssionary Andrew Vander Wagen and his wife, Effa, who was a nurse, the courageous couple who brought spiritual comfort and medical healing to the people of the frontier. Our heartfelt thanks to Elaine for the history of the Vander Wagens and her help in so many ways in researching the life of John Miller. Elaine and her husband Roger own and operate the Trading Post in Halona Plaza in the village of Zuni. They are the parents of three children.

Jewel Crockett Lambson: Jewel is the daughter of Walter Crockett and his wife, Ella, who owned a ranch adjacent to the Miller Ranch and were friends and neighbors of John Miller. Miller's son, Max, lived with the Crocketts for several years. Jewel furnished much of the research about the life of John Miller, and came up with the idea that a book should be written about him, and asked me to write it. So we became partners in the publication of this book. Jewel is the owner of two pictures of John Miller when he was a rancher in the Zuni Mountains.

Bill Crockett: Bill Crockett is the youngest son of Walter Crockett. Bill arranged for an interview with Max Miller at Crockett's bar on the road to Fence Lake between the Zuni and Navajo Reservations. Without Bill's help there would have been no stories from John Miller's son, Max Miller, and no John Miller stories from Bill Crockett. Thanks Bill, for your help, your hospitality and your many kindnesses.

Herman and Feliz Bustamante: "Muchas gracias, Feliz Bustamante y Herman Bustamante . . . por todo." I thank Feliz Bustamante and her son Herman for the time and patience they gave to help with the story of John and Isadora Miller. I especially want to thank them for allowing me to use the picture of John and Isadora taken just before the Millers left the Miller homestead for a new life in Arizona. I thank Herman for arranging the interviews with his mother and for his help in many ways. The contribution of Feliz and Herman is important, not only for this book, but for the history of the unique relationships that existed between the Mexican and Anglo settlers and the Indian tribes on the Western Frontier.

Wilfred and Bertha Ashcroft: The Ashcrofts operate a mini-farm on the outskirts of Los Lunas, New Mexico, adjacent to the beautiful Church of the Latter Day Saints which they helped build. At ninety-two, Wilfred is now quite deaf, but mentally alert, and his wife Bertha, is still baking bread from "scratch," meaning she cleans the wheat, grinds it, and bakes beautiful loaves which she shares with neighbors. Thanks, Wilfred and Bertha, for the story about the White Mule stills, and for your help and suggestions.

Keith and Sheryl Clawson: I thank Keith and Sheryl for making available the frontier pictures taken by Keith's grandfather Lewis Kirk, for Keith's invaluable help with the story of his ancestors of the Frontier, and for the story of Jesus Eriacho. I want to thank Keith and Sheryl Clawson for being friendly, helpful and hospitable people.

Katherine Eriacho: My thanks to Katherine Eriacho and her daughters for their help in obtaining the story of Jesus Eriacho. I am grateful for their consideration and polite answers to the questions I asked about Jesus, and for Katherine's story about her father and her approval of my use of the picture of Jesus.

Chimeco Eriacho: I thank Chimeco Eriacho, great-grandson of Jesus Eriacho, for sending the research story from the writings of his talented daughter, the late Lynora Eriacho, who at the age of twenty-one was killed in a tragic automobile accident. Lynora was interested in researching the history of her ancestor of Mexican descent, Jesus Eriacho.

The Bonds: I thank the late Atheling Bond and his daughter, Isabel Mangum, for the taped interview in 1979. The Bond story is essential for any history of the Life of John Miller. Thanks also to Atheling's grandson, David Vance Bond and his wife, Linda, for their help and suggestions.

Madeline Leverton: Thanks Madeline, for helping me with the Atheling Bond interview, and for an unforgettable weekend doing research and enjoying the beautiful Ramah-Zuni Mountains in your luxurious motor home.

Gary Tietjen: Gary Tietjen sent in a story about John Miller and the outlaws and also the story of his grandmother's encounter with Billy the Kid in Ramah. Tietjen's excellent book, *Encounter with the Frontier*, was indispensable, and I thank Gary for allowing me to quote from it at length.

Robert (Swede) Lambson: The late Robert Lambson arranged the interview with his father, Eugene Lambson, which surely will rank as one of the most valuable historical accounts of the life of John Miller, alias Billy the Kid. My thanks also to Swede for driving Jewel and me the long distance over rough roads to the home of Max Miller at Borrego Pass for an interview with Max.

Max Miller: How can I ever thank the late Max Miller enough for his cooperation and for the story he told about his parents' escape from Fort Sumner to Ramah? The interviews with Max were difficult for him because he was old and deaf and because he had an inherent reluctance to talk about the deceased, a characteristic of many Indians. However, Max also knew that his father, John Miller, wanted parts of his life as Billy the Kid revealed after his death. Max tried to do it the best he could. I am deeply grateful to Max Miller.

Deborah Robinson: Deborah is the sculptress who made the wax figure of Billy the Kid and aged it to show a likeness of John Miller. I thank Deborah for sending the photographs of her work and allowing me to include it in this book. Good luck Deborah, in your efforts to establish a wax museum of historical New Mexico figures. The wax museum, under the New Mexico Heritage Foundation, will certainly be important educationally, and will arouse the public in general, and young folks in particular to a real interest in the accurate history of New Mexico.

Gordon H. Muir: I thank Gordon Muir of Hamilton, Ontario, Canada, for sending the photographs of Billy the Kid's gun and holster which John Miller gave to the Canadian policeman, Frank Burrard Creasy. I also thank Dan Bartie of Toronto, who owns the gun, and who made it available.

Ken Howard: With great patience and understanding, Ken ushered me into the bright new world of the computer. Besides being a great teacher, Ken is also a computer genius! My heartfelt and grateful thanks to Ken Howard.

James Airy: James was helpful in editing this book, and is responsible for writing and researching the life of Billy the Kid (Chapter 2). James also took time from his busy life to help me with interviews and research. I thank my son, James, for standing by.

Fred Airy: I thank my late husband, Fred Airy, for his constant encouragement and help in numerous ways, for his help with photographs, layout, editing, and for assisting with as many interviews as possible in spite of failing health.

Patricia Airy Webster: Thanks to my daughter, Patricia, for taking time out from her busy life caring for six children and teaching school, to spend time helping me with interviews and editing.

Robert Barron: I am greatly indebted to Bob Barron for the research on the life of John Miller in Arizona. Bob Barron is a meticulous and scientific researcher who donates his findings to writers, libraries, and museums—all at his own expense. Bob was honest in telling me that he intended to try to prove that John Miller was not Billy the Kid. I agreed to furnish leads from the research I had conducted in the Ramah-Zuni area. Bob Barron did not prove that Miller was not the Kid, but he is still not convinced that he was. Bob is a hard man to convince, but I thank him anyway. His careful research has been very helpful.

Ray and Mary Offord: My very special thanks to my long-time friends from Stevenage, England. Mary and Ray spent a great part of their holiday in the United States to help me with wind-up interviews and photographs in Zuni, Prescott and Buckeye.

John Viebranz: Thanks to my long-time friend, John Viebranz, for taking time out from his busy life as a writer, lawyer, and inn-keeper, to ruthlessly edit the manuscript of *Whatever Happened to Billy the Kid*. John has been a big help.

Ramah-Zuni: Thanks to the people who are inhabitants of the villages of Ramah and Zuni for their friendliness, hospitality, and help in research for this book. If John and Isadora Miller had searched the world over, they could not have found better neighbors than the people who live in the spectacularly beautiful Ramah-Zuni mountain area.

Buckeye/Liberty: I want to thank Ethel Conley, Joe Conley, Carl Baxter, Nellie Dixon, Georgie Jackson, and Ruby Page from the Buckeye/Liberty communities in Arizona for helping Robert Barron and me research the later years of the life of John Miller in Arizona.

Vicki Ahl of Sunstone Press: Vicki was responsible for shepherding *Whatever Happened to Billy the Kid* through the publishing process. I thank Vicki for being patient with my last minute corrections, changes and second thoughts, and I thank her for being a knowledgeable and professional publisher.

Pat D'Aloe: I thank Pat because he is a very fine professional artist who offered to design the front cover of the book. Pat also proof-read the manuscript for typos and mistakes, not once, but twice. If there *are* any typos in this book it is not Pat's fault.

174

On Next Page:

This is a photograph of the famous Colt 45 Serial Number 60566, worn by John Miller (alias Billy the Kid) and given as a gift out of friendship and respect by him to Frank Burrard Creasy.

The gift was made after Miller had told Creasy he was Billy the Kid, and just before Creasy left for volunteer service with the Royal Canadian Dragoons as they went forth to serve the cause and defense of freedom in World War I. This gun toured the U.S.A. for years with the accompanying identification "The gun of Billy the Kid."

Courtesy of Gordon H. Muir, Richard Sonny Olmstead, photographer, and special thanks to Daniel T. Bartie of Victoria, British Columbia, owner, and Mr. Raymon J. Zyla of Mohawk Arms Inc. Utica, N.Y.